Pathway
Advanced

Vorschläge für Klausuren

Herausgegeben von:
Iris Edelbrock

Erarbeitet von:
Katharina Einhoff
Alexandra Peschel

Sprachlich betreut von:
Elin Arbin

Begleitmaterialien zum Lehrwerk für Schülerinnen und Schüler

Pathway Advanced Audio-CDs
4 CDs mit Hörtexten und Songs, Transkripte im Booklet
Best.-Nr. 062761-0

Pathway Advanced Abi *kompakt*
Thematic Vocabulary – Important Facts – Relevant Skills
Best.-Nr. 040184-5

Pathway Advanced Teacher's Manual
Best.-Nr. 040184-5

Pathway Advanced Comprehension
Reading – Listening – Viewing. Kopiervorlagen für neue Aufgabenformate
Best.-Nr. 040186-9

westermann GRUPPE

© 2018 Bildungshaus Schulbuchverlage
Westermann Schroedel Diesterweg Schöningh Winklers GmbH, Braunschweig
www.westermann.de

Das Werk und seine Teile sind urheberrechtlich geschützt.
Jede Nutzung in anderen als den gesetzlich zugelassenen bzw. vertraglich zugestandenen Fällen bedarf der vorherigen schriftlichen Einwilligung des Verlages. Nähere Informationen zur vertraglich gestatteten Anzahl von Kopien finden Sie auf www.schulbuchkopie.de.
Für Verweise (Links) auf Internet-Adressen gilt folgender Haftungshinweis:
Trotz sorgfältiger inhaltlicher Kontrolle wird die Haftung für die Inhalte der externen Seiten ausgeschlossen. Für den Inhalt dieser externen Seiten sind ausschließlich deren Betreiber verantwortlich. Sollten Sie daher auf kostenpflichtige, illegale oder anstößige Inhalte treffen, so bedauern wir dies ausdrücklich und bitten Sie, uns umgehend per E-Mail davon in Kenntnis zu setzen, damit beim Nachdruck der Verweis gelöscht wird.

Druck A^2 / Jahr 2020
Alle Drucke der Serie A sind im Unterricht parallel verwendbar.

Umschlaggestaltung: Nora Krull, Bielefeld
Umschlagabbildung: © John R. Rogers Photography, © stock.adobe.com/VladBrik
Druck und Bindung: Westermann Druck GmbH, Braunschweig

ISBN 978-3-14-**040187**-6

Contents

Listening (Hörverstehen)

1 S. 5	**Listening Comprehension** **Part A:** The Young Turks (TYT), Starbucks Ends Controversial "Race Together" Campaign, TV discussion (04:14 mins) **Part B:** Barack Obama, Selma Speech, 7 March 2015 (04:59 mins)	USA/race relations ☆
2 S. 14	**Listening Comprehension** **Part A:** Theresa May: Speech at Lancaster House, 17 January 2017 (political speech; excerpt; 04:32 mins) **Part B:** Theresa May: Speech at Lancaster House, 17 January 2017 (political speech, excerpt, 05:54 mins)	UK/Brexit

Comprehension + Analysis

3 S. 23	**Part A: Comprehension:** Rosemary Bennett: Longer Hours, More Stress? Welcome to the Digital World (newspaper article, 476 words) **Part B: Analysis:** An Office with a Sea View (photo)	Media
4 S. 28	**Part A: Comprehension:** Rana Foroohar: Starbucks for America (magazine article, 599 words) **Part B: Analysis:** Michelle Obama: On Success (quote)	USA/American Dream/race relations/economy ☆
5 S. 33	**Part A: Comprehension:** David Robson: How Important Is Social Class in Britain Today? (online article, 601 words) **Part B: Analysis:** David Robson: How Important Is Social Class in Britain Today? (online article, 601 words)	UK/social class/social success
6 S. 38	**Part A: Comprehension:** May Bulman: Brexit: People Voted to Leave EU Because They Feared Immigration, Major Survey Finds (newspaper article, 587 words) **Part B: Analysis:** Christo Kormanitski: Immigration to Great Britain (cartoon)	UK/Brexit/immigration

Comprehension + Mediation

7 S. 43	**Part A: Comprehension:** Royal Reform: The Royal Family Must Modernise in Order to Endure (newspaper article, 565 words) **Part B: Mediation:** Benedikt Schulz: 65. Thronjubiläum der Queen – „Die einzig intakte Institution" (radio interview, 630 words)	UK/monarchy
8 S. 50	**Part A: Comprehension:** Danny Strong: The Butler (screenplay, 574 words) **Part B: Mediation:** Frank Herrmann: Die wütenden Staaten von Amerika (newspaper article, 370 words)	USA/American Dream/race relations ☆
9 S. 56	**Part A: Comprehension:** Josh Jacobs, Reeva Misra: The Inconvenient Truth Behind India's Growth Story (online article/blog post, 614 words) **Part B: Mediation:** SOS Kinderdörfer: Kinderarbeit in Indien: Fakten zur wirtschaftlichen Ausbeutung von Kindern (online article, 526 words)	India/economy/child labour
10 S. 62	**Part A: Comprehension:** Dr Daniel Kenealy: How Did We Get here? A Brief History of Britain's Membership of the EU (blog post, 604 words) **Part B: Mediation:** Jens-Peter Marquardt: Großbritannien und Europa: Schon immer ein bisschen außen vor (online article, 387 words)	UK/European Union

Comprehension + Composition

11 S. 67	**Part A: Comprehension:** Mike Hercheval: Why Online Retailers Continue to Open Brick-and-Mortar Stores (comment/blog post, 471 words) **Part B: Composition:** Describe and interpret the visual. Caritas: Far Away Is Closer Than You Think	Globalization/consumption/Internet	
12 S. 72	**Part A:** Comprehension Hank Sanders, Faya Rose Toure: Still Waiting in Selma (newspaper article, 503 words) **Part B: Composition:** Write a Letter to the Editor.	USA/civil rights/American Dream	☆
13 S. 77	**Part A: Comprehension:** Ethnic Minorities: Breaking Out (magazine article, 468 words) **Part B: Composition:** Comment on the integration process of immigrants.	UK/multiculturalism	☆
14 S. 82	**Part A: Comprehension:** How Americanisms Are Killing the English Language (online article, 674 words) **Part B: Composition:** Discuss whether the German language needs to be protected by the German Constitution	The English language	

Appendix
Richtlinien für die fachspezifische Beurteilung und Bewertung
1. Aufgabenarten und Aufgabenformate   87
2. Bewertungstabelle für Listening Comprehension (Hörverstehen)   88
3. Kriterientabelle für die Vergabe von Verrechnungspunkten für die sprachliche Leistung   89
4. Kriterientabelle für die Vergabe von Verrechnungspunkten für die inhaltliche Leistung   90
5. Ermittlung des Gesamtergebnisses/Umrechnung von Verrechnungspunkten in Notenpunkte   91

Anm.: Die mit einem Stern (☆) versehenen Klausurvorschläge eignen sich auch als Klausuraufgaben in Verbindung mit dem Schwerpunktthema *The Ambiguity of Belonging*.

Topic: The American Dream – Reveries and Realities

Skills: Listening comprehension (30 points)

Part A: The Young Turks (TYT), Starbucks Ends Controversial "Race Together" Campaign, TV discussion (04:14 mins)
Part B: Barack Obama, Selma Speech, 7 March 2015 (04:59 mins)

Part A: Listening Comprehension

The Young Turks (TYT)

Starbucks Ends Controversial "Race Together" Campaign

The Young Turks (TYT) is an American liberal news programme that focuses on various political and social issues and is broadcast exclusively via its YouTube channel. The show is hosted by Cenk Uygur and Ana Kasparian.

www.youtube.com/watch?v=ilSU9ENNRZQ, 28 March 2015, 04:14 mins [04.04.2015]

ASSIGNMENTS

Listen to the text and do the following tasks.

1. **Tick the correct statement.** ____/1 VP

   The Starbucks' "Race Together" campaign involved

   ☐ launching an advertising campaign on radio and TV.

   ☐ advertising on Facebook, Twitter and Instagram.

   ☐ labelling their coffee cups with the hashtag "Race Together".

   ☐ organizing talks about race relations in their coffee shops.

2. **Complete the sentence.** ____/2 VP

   With the "Race Together" campaign, Starbucks aimed to _____

   and to _____

3. **Complete the sentence.** ____/3 VP

   People come to coffee shops like Starbucks to _____

   and _____

   not to _____

4. **True or false? Tick the correct box.** ____/2 VP

	True	False
The campaign was widely praised.	☐	☐
Some people thought about boycotting Starbucks.	☐	☐
Starbucks had expected the people's reaction.	☐	☐
Starbucks worried about losing customers.	☐	☐

5. Tick the correct statement. ____/1 VP

Some people thought the Starbucks campaign was

☐ innovative.

☐ brave.

☐ overdue.

☐ revolutionary.

6. Tick the two correct statements. ____/2 VP

Starbucks was applauded for

☐ planning to employ more minorities.

☐ stopping the campaign.

☐ launching more coffee shops in racially mixed areas.

☐ including their baristas in their campaign.

☐ apologizing to their customers for the campaign.

7. Complete the sentence. ____/1 VP

According to some people, Starbucks didn't achieve its ultimate aim because _____

_____

8. Tick the correct statement. ____/1 VP

Starbucks has been criticized for

☐ not having set out a long-term strategy for their campaign.

☐ not having integrated people involved in the Ferguson protests when conducting their campaign.

☐ trying to gain profit from the Ferguson protests.

☐ being insensitive to people's feelings about race.

9. True or false? Tick the correct box. ____/2 VP

	True	False
The campaign risks dividing people even more.	☐	☐
Starbucks will most likely lose customers.	☐	☐
Looking back, Starbucks regrets having launched the campaign.	☐	☐
Starbucks is planning to continue its campaign in a more effective way.	☐	☐

Total: ____ / 15 VP

Part A: Listening Comprehension – Transcript

The Young Turks (TYT)

Starbucks Ends Controversial "Race Together" Campaign

Ana Kasparian:
Starbucks is deciding to end a portion of their race awareness campaign where they are putting the hashtag "Race Together" on coffee cups.
Now, there is a lot of controversy, this huge kerfuffle over this issue. They wanted to not only raise awareness about race relations here in the United States, but they also wanted to basically put people on notice and let them know that Starbucks as a company is going to be much more inclusive in their hiring process; they want to start a dialogue about race in the country.
Now, people did not take kindly to this campaign. They thought that it was strange for baristas to get involved; they thought it was strange for baristas to use that hashtag on coffee cups. A lot of people go to Starbucks with the intention of studying or writing or just relaxing and so they felt like this wasn't the proper forum in order to have this conversation.
Now, Howard Schultz, who is the CEO of Starbucks, did speak to the press about this and some of the backlash and here's what he had to say:
"While there has been criticism of the initiative – and I know this hasn't been easy for any of you [speaking to his employees] – let me assure you that we didn't expect universal praise."
Well, it's good that he didn't expect that because a lot of people absolutely hated this campaign. One person said the following:
"Most people come to Starbucks for coffee. Race is an uncomfortable thing to bring up, especially in a Starbucks." (Ninette Musili)
Another person said:
"They're here for coffee. They're not here to push their political agenda. I even contemplated not coming here because of it. There are other ways you can go about doing things to stimulate interest in what you're doing. They must be doing so well they don't have to worry about losing customers over that." (Shane Mulholland)

Cenk Uygur:
Okay, so conventional wisdom is – this was a flop; it was a bad idea and they shouldn't have done it in the first place – and they realized now that they shouldn't have – that's why they are stopping. So, Starbucks says, 'It's not true, we had already planned to stop on March 22nd [2015], we just didn't announce that earlier.'
That part of the story I don't really care about, if you know they decided to stop now or earlier, so what, right? …
Here's what I do care about:
I actually really applaud them for doing it. I'm not in the camp that thinks it was stupid and goofy. Don't get me wrong. Like Howard Schultz said, it's really hard, and it might have actually cost them some customers, and it is uncomfortable. But – look at the bravery of a corporation to do that and to do it with good intent, right? Knowing that they might lose customers, knowing that they're gonna get blown apart.
You think they didn't know, when they put the hashtag "Race Together", that people were gonna make fun of them – and like they … it didn't occur to them that having a conversation with your barista about race is a little awkward. Like, they knew that was coming. And they tackled it anyway. Even if this isn't a shining success, at this moment, when you look at it in a short-term way, it's at least them trying to do the right thing by getting people to push past that uncomfortableness to have that conversation. I think it's phenomenal.

Ana Kasparian:
I applaud them for wanting to hire more minorities, I applaud them for wanting to open up stores in areas that have more minorities living there. But at the same time, I think that this kind of falls short of sparking an important dialogue, right? So, what has happened so far – from them using this hashtag on coffee cups? Absolutely nothing.
No one's had a discussion. If anything, people have just criticized Starbucks and that's it.

50 And so, I think that this was the initial phase of them publicizing something good that they're gonna do, but they could have publicized it in a more effective way.

And also, you know, because of the timing, people are criticizing them because of the Ferguson protest and they think that they're kind of exploiting that or capitalizing on that. I can understand that criticism and it could be a valid criticism. But nonetheless, I … if they used what hap-
55 pened in Ferguson to spark a dialogue about race, then I'm in favour of it. I just don't think that this component of their campaign was really successful.

Cenk Uygur:
Yeah, I don't believe that it was opportunistic at all. If anything, it's gonna polarize people and cost them customers and they did it anyway because they thought it was the right thing to do.
60 To criticize them on the heels of Ferguson is insane if you are on the issue of civil rights and on that side of the ledger. You want people to talk about it and this is a perfect time to talk about it.
(841 words)

www.youtube.com/watch?v=ilSU9ENNRZQ, 28 March 2015, transcribed by Iris Edelbrock [04.04.2015]

Part A: Listening Comprehension – Solutions

ASSIGNMENTS

Aufgabe	Lösungen	VP
1	Ausschließlich angekreuzt: ☒ labelling their coffee cups with the hashtag "Race Together".	1
2	Zwei der folgenden Aspekte sinngemäß genannt: – to raise awareness about race relations in the United States. – to let people know that Starbucks is going to hire more minorities. – to start a dialogue about race.	2
3	In den ersten zwei Lücken zwei der folgenden Aspekte sinngemäß genannt: – to have a coffee – to study – to write – to relax. In der dritten Lücke einen der folgenden Aspekte sinngemäß genannt: …, **not** to – talk about race – talk about any serious issues.	3
4	Für je zwei passend angekreuzte Aussagen 1 VP: true false The campaign was widely praised. ☐ ☒ Some people thought about boycotting Starbucks. ☒ ☐ Starbucks had expected the people's reaction. ☒ ☐ Starbucks worried about losing customers. ☐ ☒	2
5	Ausschließlich angekreuzt: ☒ brave.	1
6	Ausschließlich angekreuzt: ☒ planning to employ more minorities. ☒ launching more coffee shops in racially mixed areas.	2
7	Sinngemäß ergänzt: … it hasn't sparked any discussion/dialogue about race relations/because nothing has actually happened.	1
8	Ausschließlich angekreuzt: ☒ trying to gain profit from the Ferguson protests.	1
9	Für je zwei passend angekreuzte Aussagen 1 VP: true false The campaign risks dividing people even more. ☒ ☐ Starbucks will most probably lose customers. ☒ ☐ Looking back, Starbucks regrets having launched the campaign. ☐ ☒ Starbucks is planning to continue its campaign in a more effective way. ☐ ☒	2

Part B: Listening Comprehension

Barack Obama

Selma Speech

On 7 March 2015, Barack Obama honoured the civil rights activists who marched across the Edmund Pettus Bridge in Selma, Alabama 50 years earlier.
In 1965, Alabama police clubbed down non-violent marchers who were crossing the bridge en route to Montgomery, Alabama's state capital. This brutal crackdown on the civil rights protestors, known as Bloody Sunday, helped to pave the way for the Voting Rights Act of 1965.

www.youtube.com/watch?v=7SoG4KZOvRc, 24:24 – 27:07, 28:44 – 31:00

Annotations

Lewis and Clark (Meriwether Lewis and William Clark) led the first American expedition from St. Louis, Missouri to the Pacific Coast (1804 – 1806) on behalf of President Thomas Jefferson ■ **Sacajawea:** Native American woman who accompanied the Lewis and Clark expedition as an interpreter and guide ■ **Sojourner Truth** (1797 – 1883) African-American abolitionist and women's rights activist ■ **Fanny Lou Hamer** (1917 – 1977) African-American voting rights activist and civil rights leader ■ **Susan B. Anthony** (1820 – 1906) American social reformer and feminist who played a crucial role in women obtaining the right to vote ■ **Rio Grande** large river in Texas that forms part of the border between the U.S. and Mexico ■ **John Lewis** (*1940) African-American politician and civil rights leader

ASSIGNMENTS

Listen to the text and do the following tasks.

1. Tick the correct statement. ____/1 VP

According to Obama, the U.S. went through a lot of changes in the last half-century, e. g.

☐ waves of immigrants.

☐ fashion trends.

☐ economic recessions.

☐ technological advances.

2. Complete the sentence. ____/1 VP

Loving and believing in America means _____

_____

3. True or false? Tick the correct box. ____/2 VP

	True	False
America has endured enough changes.	☐	☐
The American system of government relies on the people.	☐	☐
American people take their rights for granted.	☐	☐
The pioneer spirit is instilled in the American people.	☐	☐

4. Complete the sentence. ___/2 VP

The U.S. is a nation of immigrants who came to America in order to _____

and to _____

5. Complete. ___/3 VP

What did the following groups of people do to build and shape the U.S.?

Slaves: _____

Ranch hands and cowboys: _____

Laborers: _____

6. Tick the two correct statements. ___/2 VP

Obama describes the U.S. as

☐ proud.

☐ fragile.

☐ independent.

☐ energetic.

☐ diverse.

☐ self-reliant.

7. Complete the sentence. ___/2 VP

Obama characterizes the young generation as _____

and _____ .

8. True or false? Tick the correct box. ___/2 VP

	True	False
The U.S. is facing too many challenges.	☐	☐
Obama calls upon young people to help improve the U.S.	☐	☐
The U.S. needs strong leadership.	☐	☐
The U.S. always strives for improvement.	☐	☐

Total: ___/ 15 VP

Part B: Listening Comprehension – Transcript

Barack Obama

Selma Speech

[…] Fellow marchers, so much has changed in fifty years. We've endured war, and fashioned peace. We've seen technological wonders that touch every aspect of our lives, and take for granted convenience our parents might scarcely imagine. But what has not changed is the imperative of citizenship, that willingness of a 26 year-old deacon, or a Unitarian minister, or a young mother of five, to decide they loved this country so much that they'd risk everything to realize its promise.

That's what it means to love America. That's what it means to believe in America. That's what it means when we say America is exceptional.

For we were born of change. We broke the old aristocracies, declaring ourselves entitled not by bloodline, but endowed by our Creator with certain unalienable rights. We secure our rights and responsibilities through a system of self-government, of and by and for the people. That's why we argue and fight with so much passion and conviction, because we know our efforts matter. We know America is what we make of it.

We are Lewis and Clark* and Sacajawea* – pioneers who braved the unfamiliar, followed by a stampede of farmers and miners, entrepreneurs and hucksters. That's our spirit.

We are Sojourner Truth* and Fannie Lou Hamer*, women who could do as much as any man and then some; and we're Susan B. Anthony*, who shook the system until the law reflected that truth. That's our character.

We're the immigrants who stowed away on ships to reach these shores, the huddled masses yearning to breathe free – Holocaust survivors, Soviet defectors, the Lost Boys of Sudan. We are the hopeful strivers who cross the Rio Grande* because they want their kids to know a better life. That's how we came to be.

We're the slaves who built the White House and the economy of the South. We're the ranch hands and cowboys who opened the West, and countless laborers who laid rail, and raised skyscrapers, and organized for workers' rights. […]

That's what America is. Not stock photos or airbrushed history or feeble attempts to define some of us as more American as others. We respect the past, but we don't pine for it. We don't fear the future; we grab for it. America is not some fragile thing; we are large, in the words of Whitman, containing multitudes. We are boisterous and diverse and full of energy, perpetually young in spirit. That's why someone like John Lewis* at the ripe age of 25 could lead a mighty march.

And that's what the young people here today and listening all across the country must take away from this day. You are America. Unconstrained by habits and convention. Unencumbered by what is, and ready to seize what ought to be. For everywhere in this country, there are first steps to be taken, and new ground to cover, and bridges to be crossed. And it is you, the young and fearless at heart, the most diverse and educated generation in our history, who the nation is waiting to follow.

Because Selma shows us that America is not the project of any one person.

Because the single most powerful word in our democracy is the word "We." We the People. We Shall Overcome. Yes We Can. It is owned by no one. It belongs to everyone. Oh, what a glorious task we are given, to continually try to improve this great nation of ours. […]

(572 words)

www.bloomberg.com/politics/articles/2015-03-07/transcript-of-president-obama-s-selma-speech [04.04.2015]

Part B: Listening Comprehension – Solutions

ASSIGNMENTS

Aufgabe	Lösungen	VP
1	Ausschließlich angekreuzt: ☒ technological advances.	1
2	Sinngemäß ergänzt: … risking everything to realize the nation's promise/… fighting for one's rights and responsibilities with conviction and passion.	1
3	Für je zwei passend angekreuzte Aussagen 1 VP: true false America has endured enough changes. ☐ ☒ The American system of government relies on the people. ☒ ☐ American people take their rights for granted. ☐ ☒ The pioneer spirit is instilled in the American people. ☒ ☐	2
4	Sinngemäß ergänzt: … to be free *and* to offer their children a better life.	2
5	Sinngemäß ergänzt: *Slaves:* built the White House and the economy of the South. *Ranch hands and cowboys:* opened the West. *Laborers:* laid the rails/built skyscrapers/organized for workers' rights.	3
6	Ausschließlich angekreuzt: ☒ energetic. ☒ diverse.	2
7	Sinngemäß zwei der folgenden Eigenschaften genannt: without limits/not restrained by anything/fearless at heart/most diverse generation in our history/most educated generation in our history	2
8	Für je zwei passend angekreuzte Aussagen 1 VP: true false The U.S. is facing too many challenges. ☐ ☒ Obama calls upon young people to help improve the U.S. ☒ ☐ The U.S. needs strong leadership. ☐ ☒ The U.S. always strives for improvement. ☒ ☐	2

Topic: Great Britain Leaving the European Union/Brexit

Skills: Listening Comprehension (political speech) (30 points)

Listening Comprehension: Theresa May: Speech at Lancaster House, 17 January 2017
Part A: 0:00 – 4:32 mins (political speech; excerpts)
Part B: 33:43 – 39:37 mins

Part A: Listening Comprehension

ASSIGNMENTS

This speech by British Prime Minister Theresa May is about the reasons for and consequences of Brexit.
It was delivered at Lancaster House on 17 January 2017. You will now hear the beginning of the speech.

1. Complete the sentence. ____/1 VP

To create a brighter future for the British, the government will have to do more than

_____

2. True or false? Tick the correct box. ____/2 VP

After Brexit Theresa May wants the United Kingdom to …

	True	False
… be a home for pensioners and invalids.	☐	☐
… send away international talent.	☐	☐
… be a truly global Britain.	☐	☐
… develop relationships with old friends and new allies.	☐	☐

3. Fill in the gaps. ____/2 VP

Theresa May wants Britain to be a _____

that is respected around the world and strong, _____

at home.

4. True or false? Tick the correct box. ____/2 VP

The government's plan for Britain …

	True	False
… will be good for foreign affairs and for ordinary British citizens.	☐	☐
… will bring true economic and social reform.	☐	☐
… will build a stronger economy and a fairer society.	☐	☐
… will show how to use the special situation of Brexit.	☐	☐

5. Tick the correct statement. ____/1 VP

Theresa May says the British can only profit from their future opportunities …

☐ … when they closely cooperate with the European Union.
☐ … when they get together with other nations and people.
☐ … when they get together with the nations and people of the Commonwealth.
☐ … when the United Kingdom and its people come together as a country.

6. Complete the sentence. ____/1 VP

Britiain's history and culture is _____.

7. True or false? Tick the correct box. ____/2 VP

Great Britain is a country …

	True	False
… that has always valued European and international relationships.	☐	☐
… whose citizens have many close friends and relatives across the world.	☐	☐
… that is proud of its European heritage.	☐	☐
… that is still among the members of the European Union.	☐	☐

8. Fill in the gaps. ____/2 VP

At the moment Britain is planning _____ for 2018, which is a reminder of Britain's unique and proud _____.

Total: ____/ 12 VP

Part B: Listening Comprehension

ASSIGNMENTS

You will now hear another part of Theresa May's speech.

1. True or false? Tick the correct box. ____/2 VP

Theresa May is confident that …

	True	False
… a new military partnership can be formed.	☐	☐
… her aims conform to what the EU and its member states need.	☐	☐
… most European countries want a good relationship with Britain after Brexit.	☐	☐
… most leaders of EU member states are interested in talks with Britain.	☐	☐

2. Fill in the gaps. ____/2 VP

With regard to the economy, Britain wants a _____

_____

but not a _____.

3. Tick the correct statement. ____/1 VP

The British want …

☐ … the EU to be a success and her future member states to do well.

☐ … the EU to be a success and the EU member states to do well.

☐ … the Euro to be a success and the EU member states to do well.

☐ … the Single Market to be a success and the EU member states to do well.

4. True or false? Tick the correct box. ____/2 VP

Free trade between Britain and the EU …

	True	False
… will be profitable for both sides.	☐	☐
… will create more jobs and wealth in the end.	☐	☐
… prevents a zero growth of the economy.	☐	☐
… prevents the erection of new barriers.	☐	☐

5. Fill in the gaps. ____/2 VP

Cooperation between Britain and the EU is needed when it comes to

_____

and _____.

6. True or false? Tick the correct box. ____/2 VP

British intelligence services …

	True	False
… are the best in Europe.	☐	☐
… have defended the safety and security of all British citizens.	☐	☐
… have helped Britain's neighbours in every way.	☐	☐
… have helped to prevent terrorist attacks in all of Europe.	☐	☐

7. True or false? Tick the correct box. ____/2 VP

Theresa May warns that the EU member states punishing Britain…

	True	False
… would not be an acceptable approach.	☐	☐
… will never happen.	☐	☐
… would be a bad deal for Britain.	☐	☐
… would have very negative consequences for the EU member states.	☐	☐

8. Tick the correct statement. ____/1 VP

No deal would be better than a bad deal because …

☐ … Britain would still be able to do business with Europe and the rest of the world.

☐ … Britain would be attractive for the best companies and biggest investors.

☐ … it would set up new trade barriers with the biggest economies in the world.

☐ … it would disrupt supply chains within the EU.

9. True or false? Tick the correct box. ____/2 VP

If there was no deal, important sectors of the EU economy would suffer …

	True	False
… because Britain is an important market for the EU car industry.	☐	☐
… because it would harm French farmers and Spanish fishermen.	☐	☐
… because it would harm young unemployed people in Europe.	☐	☐
… because the British market guarantees millions of jobs in the EU.	☐	☐

10. Complete the sentence. ____/1 VP

Theresa May thinks that a constructive and optimistic approach to the future negotiations is _____

Total: ____/ 17 VP

Part A: Listening Comprehension – Transcript

Theresa May

Speech at Lancaster House, 17 January 2017

Part I

A little over six months ago, the British people voted for change.
They voted to shape a brighter future for our country.
They voted to leave the European Union and embrace the world.
And they did so with their eyes open: accepting that the road ahead will be uncertain at times,
but believing that it leads towards a brighter future for their children – and their grandchildren too.
And it is the job of this government to deliver it. That means more than negotiating our new relationship with the EU. It means taking the opportunity of this great moment of national change to step back and ask ourselves what kind of country we want to be.
My answer is clear. I want this United Kingdom to emerge from this period of change stronger, fairer, more united and more outward-looking than ever before. I want us to be a secure, prosperous, tolerant country – a magnet for international talent and a home to the pioneers and innovators who will shape the world ahead. I want us to be a truly global Britain – the country that goes out into the world to build relationships with old friends and new allies alike.
I want Britain to be what we have the potential, talent and ambition to be. A great, global trading nation that is respected around the world and strong, confident and united at home.
That is why this government has a plan for Britain. One that gets us the right deal abroad but also ensures we get a better deal for ordinary working people at home.
It's why that plan sets out how we will use this moment of change to build a stronger economy and a fairer society by embracing genuine economic and social reform.
Why our new modern industrial strategy is being developed, to ensure every nation and area of the United Kingdom can make the most of the opportunities ahead. Why we will go further to reform our schools to ensure every child has the knowledge and the skills they need to thrive in post-Brexit Britain. Why as we continue to bring the deficit down, we will take a balanced approach by investing in our economic infrastructure – because it can transform the growth potential of our economy, and improve the quality of people's lives across the whole country.
It's why we will put the preservation of our precious Union at the heart of everything we do. Because it is only by coming together as one great union of nations and people that we can make the most of the opportunities ahead.
The result of the referendum was not a decision to turn inward and retreat from the world.
Because Britain's history and culture is profoundly internationalist.
We are a European country – and proud of our shared European heritage – but we are also a county that has always looked beyond Europe to the wide world. That is why we are one of the most racially diverse countries in Europe, one of the most multicultural members of the European Union, and why – whether we are talking about India, Pakistan, Bangladesh, America, Australia, Canada, New Zealand, countries in Africa or those that are closer to home in Europe – so many of us have close friends and relatives from across the world.
Instinctively, we want to travel to, study in, trade with countries not just in Europe but beyond the borders of our continent. Even now as we prepare to leave the EU, we are planning for the next biennial Commonwealth Heads of Government meeting in 2018 – a reminder of our unique and proud global relationships.

http://www.telegraph.co.ukl/ne/2017/01/17/theresa-may-brexit-speech-full%2F [10.03.2018]

Part B: Listening Comprehension – Transcript

Theresa May

Speech at Lancaster House, 17 January 2017

Part II

I am confident that a deal – and a new strategic partnership between the UK and the EU – can be achieved.

This is firstly because, having held conversations with almost every leader from every single EU member state; having spent time talking to the senior figures from the European institutions, including President Tusk, President Juncker, and President Schulz, and after my Cabinet colleagues David Davis, Philip Hammond and Boris Johnson have done the same with their interlocutors, I am confident that the vast majority want a positive relationship between the UK and the EU after Brexit. And I am confident that the objectives I am setting out today are consistent with the needs of the EU and its member states.

That is why our objectives include a proposed Free Trade Agreement between Britain and the European Union, and explicitly rule out membership of the EU's Single Market. Because when the EU's leaders say they believe the four freedoms of the Single Market are indivisible, we respect that position. When the 27 member states say they want to continue their journey inside the European Union, we not only respect that fact but support it.

Because we do not want to undermine the Single Market, and we do not want to undermine the European Union. We want the EU to be a success and we want its remaining member states to prosper. And of course we want the same for Britain.

And the second reason I believe it is possible to reach a good deal is that the kind of agreement I have described today is the economically rational thing that both Britain and the EU should aim for. Because trade is not a zero sum game: more of it makes us all more prosperous. Free trade between Britain and the European Union means more trade, and more trade means more jobs and more wealth creation. The erection of new barriers of trade, meanwhile, means the reverse: less trade, fewer jobs, lower growth.

The third and final reason I believe we can come to the right agreement is that cooperation between Britain and the EU is needed not just when it comes to trade but when it comes to security too.

Britain and France are Europe's only two nuclear powers. We are the only two European countries with permanent seats on the United Nations Security Council. Britain's armed forces are a crucial part of Europe's collective defence.

And our intelligence capabilities – unique in Europe – have already saved countless lives in very many terrorist plots that have been thwarted in countries across our continent. After Brexit, Britain wants to be a good friend and neighbour in every way, and that includes defending the safety and security of all our citizens.

So I believe the framework I have outlined today is in Britain's interests. It is in Europe's interests. And it is in the interests of the wider world.

But I must be clear. Britain wants to remain a good friend and neighbour to Europe. Yet I know there are some voices calling for a punitive deal that punishes Britain and discourages other countries from taking the same path.

That would be an act of calamitous self-harm for the countries of Europe. And it would not be the act of a friend.

Britain would not – indeed we could not – accept such an approach. And while I am confident that this scenario need never arise – while I am sure a positive agreement can be reached – I am equally clear that no deal for Britain is better than a bad deal for Britain.

Because we would still be able to trade with Europe. We would be free to strike trade deals across the world. And we would have the freedom to set the competitive tax rates and embrace the policies that would attract the world's best companies and biggest investors to Britain. And

– if we were excluded from accessing the Single Market – we would be free to change the basis of Britain's economic model.

But for the EU, it would mean new barriers to trade with one of the biggest economies in the world. It would jeopardize investments in Britain by EU companies worth more than half a trillion pounds. It would mean a loss of access for European firms to the financial services of the City of London. It would risk exports from the EU to Britain worth around £290 billion every year. And it would disrupt the sophisticated and integrated supply chains upon which many EU companies rely.

Important sectors of the EU economy would also suffer. We are a crucial – profitable – export market for Europe's automotive industry, as well as sectors including energy, food and drink, chemicals, pharmaceuticals, and agriculture. These sectors employ millions of people around Europe. And I do not believe that the EU's leaders will seriously tell German exporters, French farmers, Spanish fishermen, the young unemployed of the Eurozone, and millions of others, that they want to make them poorer, just to punish Britain and make a political point.

For all these reasons – and because of our shared values and the spirit of goodwill that exists on both sides – I am confident that we will follow a better path. I am confident that a positive agreement can be reached.

It is right that the government should prepare for every eventuality – but to do so in the knowledge that a constructive and optimistic approach to the negotiations to come is in the best interests of Europe and the best interests of Britain.

http://www.telegraph.co.uk/ne/2017/01/17/theresa-mays-brexit-speech-full%2F [10.03.2018]

Part A: Listening Comprehension – Solutions

ASSIGNMENTS

Aufgabe	Lösungen			VP
1	*sinngemäß ergänzt:* negotiating our new relationship with the EU.			1
2	*für je zwei passend angekreuzte Aussagen 1 VP:* be a home to pensioners and invalids. send away international talent. be a truly global Britain. develop relationships with old friends and new allies.	true ☐ ☐ ☒ ☒	false ☒ ☒ ☐ ☐	2
3	*erste Lücke richtig ergänzt:* great global trading nation *zweite Lücke richtig ergänzt:* confident and united at home.			1 1
4	*für je zwei passend angekreuzte Aussagen 1 VP:* will be good for foreign affairs and for ordinary British citizens. will bring true economic and social reform. will build a stronger economy and a fairer society. will show how to use the special situation of Brexit.	true ☒ ☐ ☒ ☐	false ☐ ☒ ☐ ☒	2
5	*ausschließlich angekreuzt:* when the United Kingdom and its people come together as a country.			1
6	*richtig ergänzt:* profoundly internationalist.			1
7	*für je zwei passend angekreuzte Aussagen 1 VP:* that has always valued European and international relationships. whose citizens have many close friends and relatives across the world. that is proud of its European heritage. that is still among the members of the European Union.	true ☒ ☐ ☒ ☐	false ☐ ☒ ☐ ☒	2
8	*erste Lücke sinngemäß ergänzt:* the next biennial Commonwealth Heads of Government meeting *zweite Lücke richtig ergänzt:* global relationships.			1 1

Part B: Listening Comprehension – Solutions

ASSIGNMENTS

Aufgabe	Lösungen			VP
1	*für je zwei passend angekreuzte Aussagen 1 VP:*	true	false	2
	a new military partnership can be formed.	☐	☒	
	her aims conform to what the EU and its member states need.	☒	☐	
	most European countries want a good relationship with Britain after Brexit.	☒	☐	
	most leaders of EU member states are interested in talks with Britain.	☐	☒	
2	*erste Lücke richtig ergänzt:* Free Trade Agreement (between Britain and the European Union)			1
	zweite Lücke richtig ergänzt: membership in the (EU's) Single Market.			1
3	*ausschließlich angekreuzt:* the EU to be a success and the EU member states to do well.			1
4	*für je zwei passend angekreuzte Aussagen 1 VP:*	true	false	2
	will be profitable for both sides.	☒	☐	
	will create more jobs and wealth in the end.	☒	☐	
	prevents a zero growth of the economy.	☐	☒	
	prevents the erection of new barriers.	☐	☒	
5	*erste Lücke richtig ergänzt:* trade			1
	zweite Lücke richtig ergänzt: security.			1
6	*für je zwei passend angekreuzte Aussagen 1 VP:*	true	false	2
	are the best in Europe.	☒	☐	
	have defended the safety and security of all British citizens.	☐	☒	
	have helped Britain's neighbours in every way.	☐	☒	
	have helped to prevent terrorist attacks in all of Europe.	☒	☐	
7	*für je zwei passend angekreuzte Aussagen 1 VP:*	true	false	2
	would not be an acceptable approach.	☒	☐	
	will never happen.	☐	☒	
	would be a bad deal for Britain.	☐	☒	
	would have very negative consequences for the EU member states.	☒	☐	
8	*ausschließlich angekreuzt:* Britain would still be able to do business with Europe and the rest of the world.			1
9	*für je zwei passend angekreuzte Aussagen 1 VP:*	true	false	2
	because Britain is an important market for the EU car industry.	☒	☐	
	because it would harm French farmers and Spanish fishermen.	☐	☒	
	because it would harm young unemployed people in Europe.	☐	☒	
	because the British market guarantees millions of jobs in the EU.	☒	☐	
10	*sinngemäß ergänzt:* in the best interests of Europe and the best interests of Britain.			1

© Westermann Gruppe, Best.-Nr. 040187

Topic: Modern Media – Social, Smart and Spying?!

Skills: Comprehension of a non-fictional text (newspaper article) (5 points); analysis of a photo (25 points)

Part A: Comprehension: Rosemary Bennett: Longer Hours, More Stress? Welcome to the Digital World (476 words)

Part B: Analysis: A photo: The Digital Nomad Life – Combining Work and Travel

Part A: Comprehension

Rosemary Bennett

Longer Hours, More Stress? Welcome to the Digital World

Smartphones, tablets, and other digital devices have resulted in longer working hours, higher stress levels and blurred[1] boundaries between personal and working life, according to a large-scale study. It found that the digital revolution has been almost entirely negative for the health and happiness of employees. The only clear advantage identified was a greater ability to attend
5 moveable family events such as a school sports day.
These one-off events were more than out-weighed by reduced time spent with the family. Researchers at the University of Surrey examined 65 big studies on the subject, covering the experiences of about 50,000 employees. They found that handing out work phones and other gadgets to staff generally came with an expectation that employees were available for work at all times.
10 Few companies have clear policies about the limits of contacting staff in their free time, making it a virtual free-for-all.
Svenja Schlachter, a researcher at the University of Surrey, said that many more companies needed to address the issue – or face the consequences of having a burnt-out workforce.
"In the absence of a policy written down in black and white, employees tended to take guidance
15 from their manager or their colleagues. If managers sent emails late at night, staff felt they were required to answer them," she said.
"Employees generally showed great enthusiasm at first when they received phones from work but very quickly they felt an expectation was established that meant they had to be always available. They lost a sense of control and in the long-run it became a burden." [...]
20 Overall smartphone technology is thought to have led to white-collar employees[2] working an average of a full working day extra each week, and managers up to two days a week more.
Family life emerged as the greatest casualty of digital technology, with parents being often distracted or breaking off during the evening, at weekends and on holiday to deal with work emails and calls.
25 A handful of German companies have led the way in putting restrictions in place to protect the personal life of staff. Volkswagen, BMW and Puma stop their company servers from forwarding emails to staff half an hour after the end of the working day, making it clear that employees are not meant to check them at night or during weekends.
Ms Schlachter said that the research suggested that individuals dealt with interruptions to their
30 personal life in different ways, some ruminating[3] for hours over a single work email, while others simply put it to the back of their mind until the morning. However, the general trend appeared to be negative, with long-term problems for health and happiness.
She said: "Staying 'switched on' might increase flexibility and efficiency at first glance, but in the long run it can result in longer work hours and be detrimental[4] to wellbeing due to stress
35 and work-life balance issues."
The Times, 8 January 2015

[1] **blurred** vague, unclear – [2] **white-collar employee** sb. who works in an office – [3] **to ruminate** to think carefully and for a long period about sth. – [4] **detrimental** [ˌdetrɪˈmentəl] (fml.) causing harm and damage

ASSIGNMENTS

Read the text and tick the correct answers (true/false). Cite the passage in the text that proves your answer. Write down the line numbers and the first and last three words of the quotation. If the quote is less than six words, write down the full quote.

1. Digital devices at the workplace are making it increasingly difficult to draw a line between one's work and private life. true ☐ false ☐

   line(s) _____ : _____

   _____

2. The fact that digital devices enable employees to organize their schedule according to their children's activities has turned out to be a significant advantage. true ☐ false ☐

   line(s) _____ : _____

   _____

3. According to Ms Schlachter, ignoring the problems that come along with the digital revolution will backfire on the companies. true ☐ false ☐

   line(s) _____ : _____

   _____

4. Employees in higher positions generally benefit from the increased use of digital devices at the workplace. true ☐ false ☐

   line(s) _____ : _____

   _____

5. Ms Schlachter is worried about the short-term as well as the long-term consequences of the digital revolution. true ☐ false ☐

   line(s) _____ : _____

   _____

Total: _____ /5 VP

Part B: Analysis

The Digital Nomad Life: Combining Work and Travel

ASSIGNMENTS

Describe and interpret the photo. Compare the message conveyed in this photo to the message of the text "Longer Hours, More Stress? Welcome to the Digital World" by Rosemary Bennett. Comment on the opportunity to work as a digital nomad.

Part A: Comprehension – Solutions

ASSIGNMENTS

Tick the correct answers (true/false). Cite the passage in the text that proves your answer. Write down the line numbers and the first and last three words of the quotation. If the quote is less than six words, write down the full quote.

1. **Digital devices at the workplace are making it increasingly difficult to draw a line between one's work and private life.**

true ☒　false ☐

line(s) 1–2: Smartphones, tablets, and … and working life, …

2. **The fact that digital devices enable employees to organize their schedule according to their children's activities has turned out to be a significant advantage.**

true ☐　false ☒

line(s) 6: These one-off … with the family.

3. **According to Ms Schlachter, ignoring the problems that come along with the digital revolution will backfire on the companies.**

true ☒　false ☐

line(s) 12–13: Svenja Schlachter, a … a burnt-out workforce.

4. **Employees in higher positions generally benefit from the increased use of digital devices at the workplace.**

true ☐　false ☒

line(s) 20–21: Overall smartphone technology … a week more.

5. **Ms Schlachter is worried about the short-term as well as the long-term consequences of the digital revolution.**

true ☐　false ☒

line(s) 33–35: She said: "Staying … work-life balance issues."

Part B: Analysis – Solutions

ASSIGNMENT

Students are expected

- to write a short introduction mentioning
  - the type of visual (a photo),
  - the title "Frau arbeitet auf einem Kreuzfahrtschiff",
  - the general topic (e.g. working in the digital world),
  - 27th June 2016
  - taken from the Internet (iStock)

- to describe the picture referring to
  - the setting, the people and the action of the scene: a young woman is sitting on deck of a boat / cruise ship, working on her laptop computer and enjoying a cup of coffee and the view of the sea at the same time.

- to analyse the picture , i. e. they should point out similarities and differences between the message conveyed by the text and the photo.
  - The message the author of the text wants to convey is that the growing access and integration of digital devices into the working world has generally had a detrimental effect on the employees, i.e. they work longer hours, show higher stress levels, are not able anymore to differentiate between their personal and their working life and neglect their family life. As a rule, the digital workplace has resulted in a deterioration of the employees' health and happiness.
  In contrast to the text, the photo paints a totally different picture of the digital workplace and working life. The woman depicted in the photo is obviously able to successfully blend work and leisure time together. Instead of working in a confined office she is free to choose her workplace (here a boat / cruise ship) and schedule her work flexibly.
  Whereas the text refers to the negative consequences the digital working world has for families, the photo emphasizes positive aspects like freedom and a beautiful work space.

- to point out and weigh the advantages and disadvantages of being a digital nomad and eventually draw a conclusion as to its desirability. Students should take into account the downsides of being a digital nomad, i. e. an instable and unreliable lifestyle, possible difficulties in providing for one's family, loneliness, the need to organize and discipline oneself.

Topic: The American Dream – Reveries and Realities

Skills: Comprehension of a non-fictional text (newspaper article) (10 points); analysis of a quote (25 points)

Part A: Comprehension: Rana Foroohar: Starbucks for America, 2015 (599 words)

Part B: Analysis: A quote: Michelle Obama: On success

Part A: Comprehension

Rana Foroohar

Starbucks for America

From the pages of TIME

The 61-year-old Starbucks CEO[1] doesn't mind tears or hugs or displays of emotion of any kind. This is front and center[2] on an icy January afternoon in New York City, where Schultz is leading a forum on race. Shocked by recent police shootings and unrest
5 in Ferguson, Mo., New York City and Oakland, Calif., he decided to hold open meetings in five cities where Starbucks employees from top managers to entry-level baristas could speak frankly about their experiences with racism.

A little more than 40 % of the company's baristas are minorities, and the audience of 400 or so at Cooper Union's auditorium reflects that. Schultz has just come from a meeting with New
10 York City police commissioner William Bratton in which the two discussed ways the company could help ease[3] tensions. Like a candidate holding forth[4] during a televised town hall, Schultz is speaking from a spot on the floor near the crowd. "People have told me we shouldn't touch this issue, that we might stir things up, upset the shareholders. I don't agree with that," he says. "Conversations are being ignored because people are afraid to touch this issue. But if I ignore
15 this and just keep ringing the register[5], then I become part of the problem. So here we are. Let's talk."

Pretty soon, the floodgates[6] are open. The microphone is passed around, and dozens of partners, as Starbucks employees are called, begin sharing their stories. Some are crying, others angry. [...]

20 Starbucks – whose baristas, at Schultz's suggestion, wrote "come together" on coffee cups in protest over the [2013 government] shutdown[7] – already had a reputation at that point as a progressive company, having been one of the first retailers in the country to offer affordable, comprehensive health care to full-time and eligible[8] part-time employees and their families, as well as a stock-grant program[9] (Bean Stock) for all. And there have also been big pushes in areas
25 like workforce training (the company and the Schultz Family Foundation together have trained nearly 700 disadvantaged young people for jobs in retail or customer service), hiring and training of returning veterans (Starbucks has pledged to employ 10,000), student debt and access to education (the company has promised to help pay for employees to get their bachelor's degree, an investment that will likely cost Starbucks tens of millions of dollars).
30 Schultz says he is deeply invested in[10] these ideas not only because making the company a preferred employer helps keep turnover[11] costs lower and service quality higher than the industry average but also because he believes corporations have a duty to help people realize the American Dream. "I think the private sector simply has to take a larger role than they have in the past.

---

[1] **CEO** [ˌsiː iː ˈoʊ] (*abbr.*) Chief Executive Officer; the president of a large company – [2] **front and center** (*infml.*) the main focus – [3] **to ease sth.** to make sth. less severe – [4] **to hold forth** (*phr.v.*) to speak at great length about sth. – [5] **to ring the register** *die Kasse klingeln lassen* – [6] **to open the floodgates** (*infml.*) to allow many people to do sth. that was previously not allowed; here: to show emotions openly – [7] **the shutdown** here: period from 1–16 October 2013, when the Republican-controlled House of Representatives caused a shutdown of most government agencies by refusing to grant funding for the budget in protest of Obama's healthcare legislation – [8] **eligible** [ˈelɪdʒəbl] entitled, meeting certain criteria – [9] **stock-grant program** *Gratis-Aktien* – [10] **to be invested in sth.** to be deeply committed to sth. – [11] **(staff) turnover** *Mitarbeiterfluktuation*

Our responsibility goes beyond the P&L[12] and our stock price. We have to take care of people in the communities that we serve. If half the country or at least a third of the country doesn't have the same opportunities as the rest going forward, then the country won't survive. That's not socialism," says Schultz, it's practical reality. [...]

On the policy front, the company is planning to dramatically ramp up[13] the number of out-of-work younger people, veterans and other struggling groups that get workforce training through Starbucks. On Feb. 9 [2015] in L.A., Schultz is holding the company's first open forum on racism with non-Starbucks participants. Meanwhile, the early-morning emails with the next big idea – to staffers[14], friends, his wife, other CEOs – are unlikely to stop coming anytime soon. "I like to take big swings," says Schultz, smiling and chugging[15] yet another Sumatra[16]. "Maybe it's all the coffee."

Time, 16 February 2015, pp. 16 ff.

TIME and the TIME logo are registered trademarks of TIME Inc. used under license.

ASSIGNMENTS

Read the text and do the following tasks. If required, cite the passage of the text that proves your answer. Write down the line numbers an the first and last three words of the quotation. If the quote is less than six words, wirte down the full quote.

1. **Match the people with the actions and fill in the corresponding letters.** ____/4 VP
   One action cannot be attributed to any person or group.

   A. experienced racism

   B. is/are benefiting from Starbucks' social commitment to disadvantaged people

   C. initiated an open forum about racism

   D. introduced measures to fight racism at work

   E. supported Starbucks in its attempt to deal with racism

police commissioner William Bratton	Starbucks CEO Howard Schultz	Starbucks employees	veterans

2. **Tick the correct answers (true/false). Cite the passage of the text that proves your answer.** ____/4 VP

   a) The majority of the Starbucks employees come from a minority background.   true false

   line(s) _____ : _____

   _____

   b) Racially motivated offenses and incidents at Starbucks prompted CEO Schultz to organize open talks about racism.   true false

   line(s) _____ : _____

   _____

   c) CEO Schultz defiantly ignored other people's warnings to start a talk about racism.   true false

   line(s) _____ : _____

   _____

[12] **P&L** (*abbr.*) Profit and Loss; here: how much money the company makes – [13] **to ramp sth. up** (*phr.v.*) to dramatically increase sth. – [14] **staffer** (*AE*) employee – [15] **to chug sth.** *etw. auf ex trinken* – [16] **Sumatra** a dark roast coffee

   d) The talks about racism at Starbucks are very emotional.

   line(s) _____ : _____

   _____

3. **Tick the correct statement. Cite the passage of the text that proves your answer.** ____/1 VP

   According to Schultz investing in the well-being of Starbucks' employees

   ☐ … has boosted Starbucks' stock price.

   ☐ … has led to rising sales at its coffee shops.

   ☐ … has turned out to be too costly.

   ☐ … will benefit the company in various ways in the long run.

   line(s) _____ : _____

   _____

4. **Complete the following sentence using your own words or with words from the text.** ____/1 VP

   If Starbucks and other companies don't help socially disadvantaged people to achieve the

   American Dream _____

   _____

   Total: ____/10 VP

Part B: Analysis

When Michelle Obama spoke about her husband at the Democratic National Convention on 4 September 2012 she said that for her husband Barack Obama. …

„… success isn't about how much money you make; it's about the difference you make in people's lives."

ASSIGNMENT

Analyse the quote taking into consideration your knowledge of the American Dream. Then relate the quote to Howard Schultz's view that "corporations have a duty to help people realize the American Dream" (ll. 31 f.). Briefly comment on his view.

Part A: Comprehension – Solutions

ASSIGNMENTS

1. **Match the people with the actions and fill in the corresponding letters. One action cannot be attributed to any person or group.**

    A. experienced racism

    B. is/are benefiting from Starbucks' social commitment to disadvantaged people

    C. initiated an open forum about racism

    D. introduced measures to fight racism at work

    E. supported Starbucks in its attempt to deal with racism

police commissioner William Bratton	Starbucks CEO Howard Schultz	Starbucks employees	veterans
E	C	A	B

2. **Tick the correct answers (true/false). Cite the passage of the text that proves your answer.**

    a) The majority of the Starbucks employees come from a minority background. — false

    line(s) 7: A little more … baristas are minorities, …

    b) Racially motivated offenses and incidents at Starbucks prompted CEO Schultz to organize open talks about racism. — false

    line(s) 3–6: Shocked by recent … experiences with racism.

    c) CEO Schultz defiantly ignored other people's warnings to start a talk about racism. — true

    line(s) 11–15: "People have told … are. Let's talk."

    d) The talks about racism at Starbucks are very emotional. — true

    line(s) 16–17: Pretty soon, the … crying, others angry.

3. **Tick the correct statement. Cite the passage of the text that proves your answer.**

    According to Schultz investing in the well-being of Starbucks' employees …

    ☐ … has boosted Starbucks' stock price.

    ☐ … has led to rising sales at its coffee shops.

    ☐ … has turned out to be too costly.

    ☒ … will benefit the company in various ways in the long run.

    line(s) 29–30: Schultz says he … the industry average, …

4. **Complete the following sentence using your own words or with words from the text.**

    If Starbucks and other companies don't help socially disadvantaged people to achieve the American Dream

    the gap between rich and poor will widen. / the country won't survive.

Part B: Analysis – Solutions

ASSIGNMENT

Students are expected

- to briefly explain the concept of the American Dream.
  According to the original idea of the American Dream everybody has the equal and inalienable right to life, liberty and the pursuit of happiness, regardless of race, gender, social class, religion, etc. In the course of history the definition of happiness has changed, becoming associated more with materialistic values on the one hand and more idealistic values on the other. Whereas the "materialistic" American Dream is based on the acquisition of material wealth in the form of financial security, a good education and job, decent housing and health care, the "idealistic" American Dream includes e. g. leading a meaningful life, contributing to one's community and society, respecting nature, and spending time with family and friends.

- to relate the definition of the American Dream to Obama's vision of it.
  Obama's definition of being successful in life, i. e. fulfilling the American Dream, is clearly in line with the idealistic values mentioned above. It is not financial prosperity that matters, but the individual's commitment to getting involved in other people's lives in a way that enriches their own life.

- to relate Obama's idea of the American Dream to Schultz's view that "corporations have a duty to help people realize the American Dream".
  Schultz's view is similar to Obama's vision of the American Dream insofar as he is not only concerned about his company's or any individual's financial success, but also attaches great importance to caring for other people by creating equal opportunities for everybody, thereby making a difference in other people's lives. His ultimate aim is to close the gap which is gradually widening between people who are successful and those who do not have the chance to succeed. In order to do this, Starbucks is planning to employ more people who have difficulties in (re-)entering the job market, e. g. unemployed young people and veterans.

- to briefly comment on Schultz's idea of corporations actively getting involved in other people's lives instead of leaving it to the individual to take care of him or herself.

© Westermann Gruppe, Best.-Nr. 040187

Topic: The importance of class in modern Britain

Skills: Comprehension of a non-fictional text (online article) (5 points); analysis of a text (25 points)

Part A: Comprehension: David Robson: How Important Is Social Class in Britain Today? (online article, 601 words)

Part B: Analysis: David Robson: How Important Is Social Class in Britain Today? (online article, 601 words)

Part A: Comprehension

David Robson

How Important Is Social Class in Britain Today?

Like it or loathe[1] it, many see the class system as a quintessential[2] element of British life, together with our obsession for tea and cake and talking about the weather.
"Class distinctions do not die; they merely learn new ways of expressing themselves," the British sociologist Richard Hoggart once wrote. "Each decade we shiftily[3] declare we have buried class, each decade the coffin stays empty." A quick perusal[4] of the foreign media would certainly paint a picture of a rigid class system, especially compared to places like the USA where ambition, talent and elbow grease[5] are thought to be the only limits.
But how well does this stereotype really hold up? Is the British class system still as entrenched[6] as it ever was? Or are those old distinctions a thing of the past, best left behind with the corsets and top hats[7] of our period dramas[8]? These questions have been difficult to answer with any certainty, but recent data has offered some surprising insights.
[…] Considering factors like education, salary, professions, and household ownership, the BBC's own great British Class Survey discovered seven distinct classes in total, with an elite (representing roughly 6% of the population) residing above a wide spectrum of working and middle classes. Perhaps a more pertinent[9] question, then, is not whether class distinctions exist, but whether it is possible to move out of one pigeonhole[10] and into another. Just how much does your family's background influence how well you can expect to do in life? The general consensus would seem to be that social mobility has increased with improvements in education and social welfare, but is it really that clear-cut?
[…] According to a 2010 report by the Organisation for Economic Cooperation and Development, Britain is indeed among the worst countries for certain measures of social mobility, with the parents' wealth strongly influencing the child's prospects of higher education and a good salary.
Even so, there had been a steady average rise in the population after World War Two, with each child expecting to be slightly better off than their parents. Unfortunately, the relative proportions of people moving up or down a class now seems to be reversing. "More men and women are experiencing downward mobility and fewer of them experience upward mobility than before," says Erzsebet Bukodi at the University of Oxford, who calls it "the dark side of the Golden Age of Mobility" – with more people at the top, more have the potential to fall.
The trouble is, the fabric of our society has so many strands[11], it can be difficult to disentangle[12] all the potential factors that could influence your status. One potential issue is that most previous studies have only examined two generations – parents and children – whereas your class may depend on many more branches of the family tree. Tak Wing Chan at University College London, for instance, has found that a child is two-and-a-half times as likely to have a profes-

---

[1] **to loathe** to dislike strongly – [2] **quintessential** very important – [3] **shifty** smart – [4] **perusal** reading – [5] **elbow grease** hard work – [6] **entrenched** deeply rooted – [7] **top hat** *Zylinderhut* – [8] **period** drama television programme which is set in the past, *Kostümfilm* – [9] **pertinent** fitting – [10] **pigeonhole** a category, typically an overly restrictive one, to which sb. or sth. is assigned – [11] **strand** one of the different parts of an idea, a plan, a story, etc. – [12] **to disentangle** *entwirren*

35 sional or managerial job, if their grandparents were of a higher class. It could be that the grandparents pay for education, help with child care, or offer a network of contacts that could boost their grandchild's work opportunities.

With these more distant ties, social class may be even less elastic than we thought – even if one generation pulls away, the next may be tugged[13] backwards thanks to the broader connec-
40 tion of their family at large. "If you want to predict someone's outcome, you don't just look at their parents – but also their uncles and aunts, their grandparents and great-grandparents," says Gregory Clark at the University of California, Davis. "They are all predictive."

BBC – Future, 7 April 2016
http://www.bbc.com/future/story/20160406-how-much-does-social-class-matter-in-britain-today.

ASSIGNMENTS

Read the text and do the following tasks. Cite the passage of the text that proves your answer. Write down the line numbers and the first and last three words of the quotation. If the quote is less than six words, write down the full quote.

1. Tick the correct statement.

According to a British sociologist,

☐ a new class system emerges every ten years.

☐ the British regularly say there is no class system anymore but it still exists.

☐ the British want to abolish the class system every ten years but they don't.

☐ there is a symbolic burying of the class system every ten years but the coffin is just for show.

line(s) _____ : _____

_____

2. Tick the correct answer (true/false)

According to the author, it is more important to find out whether social mobility is possible than whether there are different classes.   true false
                                                                                                                                         ☐   ☐

line(s) _____ : _____

_____

3. Tick the correct answer (true/false)

It is usually said that there has been more social mobility since education and   true false
social welfare have been improved.   ☐   ☐

line(s) _____ : _____

_____

[13] **to tug** to pull

4. **Tick the correct statement.**

   A report from 2010 says that …

   ☐ … Britain is one of the worst countries when it comes to climbing the social ladder.

   ☐ … in Britain a child's success still depends on their parents' financial situation.

   ☐ … in Britain a person needs their parents' wealth to move up in society.

   ☐ … in Britain the children of wealthy parents are better at school.

   line(s) _____ : _____

   _____

5. **Tick the correct statement.**

   Tak Wing Chan found out that …

   ☐ … children like professional or managerial jobs if their grandparents are of a higher class.

   ☐ … grandparents use their Internet contacts to help their grandchildren find jobs.

   ☐ … many grandparents actively participate in their grandchildren's education.

   ☐ … the grandparents' social class influences a grandchild's professional success.

   line(s) _____ : _____

   _____

   Total: _____ /5 VP

Part B: Analysis

ASSIGNMENT

Analyse the issue of social class in Great Britain as presented in the given text.

Part A: Comprehension – Solution

ASSIGNMENTS

Read the text and do the following tasks. Cite the passage of the text that proves your answer. Write down the line numbers and the first and last three words of the quotation. If the quote is less than six words, write down the full quote.

1. **Tick the correct statement.**

    According to a British sociologist,

    ☒ the British regularly say there is no class system anymore but it still exists.

    line(s): 3 – 5: the British sociologist … coffin stays empty.

2. **Tick the correct answer (true/false)**

	true	false
According to the author it is more important to find out whether social mobility is possible than whether there are different classes.	☒	☐

    line(s): 15 – 17: Perhaps a more … and into another.

3. **Tick the correct answer (true/false)**

	true	false
It is usually said that there has been more social mobility since education and social welfare have been improved.	☒	☐

    line(s): 17 – 19: The general consensus … and social welfare

4. **Tick the correct statement.**

    A report from 2010 says that

    ☒ in Britain a child's success still depends on their parents' financial situation.

    line(s): 20 – 23: According to a … a good salary.

5. **Tick the correct statement.**

    Tak Wing Chan found out that

    ☒ the grandparents' social class influences a grandchild's professional success.

    line(s): 33 – 35: Tak Wing Chan … a higher class.

Part B: Analysis – Solution

ASSIGNMENT

Analyse the issue of social class in Great Britain as presented in the given text.
- class continues to be very important in British society
- proof: a BBC survey which considered factors such as education, wages, professions and whether a person owns property found that there were seven distinct social classes (elite class: 6 % of the population)
- as the existence of distinct social classes is indisputable, a more important issue seems to be that of social mobility
- improvements in education and social welfare have led to a higher social mobility since World War II
- but: a report by the Organisation for Economic Cooperation and Development says: the parents' wealth still influences a child's success in life
- at the moment: a reverse movement becomes obvious: more people are descending the social ladder than climbing it
- most studies in this field have only done research into two generations
- other studies have found that not only the parents but also the grandparents (and perhaps even more distant family members) determine a person's success in life
- so even if the parents have moved up the social ladder a child might be drawn back by the grandparents' (or other relatives') social position

To conclude:
Social class is still an important issue in British society and determines a person's success in life, which means social mobility is lower than in other countries. Social mobility is made more difficult by the fact that a person's success in life is not only determined by their parents but also by more distant members of the family, as recent research has shown.

> **Topic:** Reasons for Brexit
>
> **Skills:** Comprehension of a non-fictional text (online article) (5 points); analysis of a text (25 points)
>
> **Part A: Comprehension:** May Bulman: Brexit: People Voted to Leave EU Because They Feared Immigration, Major Survey Finds (newspaper article, 587 words)
>
> **Part B: Analysis:** Christo Kormanitski, Immigration to Great Britain (cartoon)

Part A: Comprehension

May Bulman

Brexit: People Voted to Leave EU Because They Feared Immigration, Major Survey Finds

Britain's vote to leave the EU was the result of widespread anti-immigration sentiment, rather than a wide dissatisfaction with politics, according to a major survey of social attitudes in the UK. Findings from the British Social Attitudes (BSA) survey published on Wednesday show Brexit was the result of widespread concern over the numbers of people coming to the UK – millions of whom have done so under the EU's freedom of movement rules in recent years. The research, collated[1] by the National Centre for Social Research through a survey of nearly 3,000 British people, states suggestions by politicians and others that the Brexit vote represented a lightning rod[2] for a general disenchantment with politics were "widely off the mark".

Nearly three-quarters (73 per cent) of those who are worried about immigration voted Leave[3], compared with 36 per cent of those who did not identify this as a concern, the research found, showing the discrepancy in views about immigration between Remain[4] and Leave voters.

It also reveals that the longer any given voter felt EU migrants should have lived in the UK before qualifying for welfare benefits, the more likely they were to vote to leave the EU.

Meanwhile 45 per cent of those who trust the Government a great deal or tend to trust it voted to leave, compared with 65 per cent of those who distrust it greatly – marking a less considerable difference and suggesting trust in politicians was less of a driving factor in the vote for Brexit.

While the survey results find that those with less interest in politics may have been a little more likely to make it to the polls than in general elections, the multivariate[5] analysis concludes that the vote was a "litmus test[6] of the merit of the EU project".

It states that for the most part, only items associated with people's sense of national identity and cultural outlook were significantly associated with vote choice, concluding that the outcome of the referendum reflected the concern of more "authoritarian", socially conservative voters in Britain about some of the social consequences of EU membership, most notably immigration.

Roger Harding, head of public attitudes at NatCen[7], told The Independent[8]: "For leave voters, the vote was particularly about immigration and the social consequences of it.

"We find a bit of correlation with people who don't trust Government, but that's not nearly as strong. Two biggest guides to why people voted leave were those most concerned with immigration and those with a lower level of education.

"On the topic of immigration itself – we found a big divide between young graduates who were positive about the social impact on immigration and older school leavers who were much more negative. The view in Britain on aggregate[9] is pretty middling, but underneath is that stark divide, and this division could be a problem for all political parties trying to win over the country post-Brexit".

---

[1] **to collate** to collect – [2] **lightning rod** a person or thing that attracts criticism, especially if the criticism is then not directed at sb./sth. else – [3] **Leave** leave the EU – [4] **Remain** remain in the EU – [5] **multivariate** *Statistik: mehrdimensionale Verteilung* – [6] **litmus test** the ultimate test; *Lackmustest* – [7] **NatCen** Britian's leading independent social research institute – [8] **The Independent** British online newspaper – [9] **on aggregate** as a whole

35 Mr Harding added that the BSA survey didn't question people directly on why they voted the way they did in the referendum, but rather assessed the correlation, which he said offered a more accurate insight.
"We didn't ask people directly why they voted the way they voted, because people aren't the best guides to how they voted", he said.
40 "We did a deeper and more accurate assessment by calculating close correlations. We found the Leave vote relates to concerns about immigration and education. Many politicians have come out and said it was all about sovereignty and other things, but our findings indicate this isn't the case".

http://www.independent.co.uk/news/uk/home-news/brexit-latest-nes-leave-eu-immigration-main-reason-european-union-survey-a7811651.html (28 June 2017) [10.03.2018]

ASSIGNMENTS

Read the text and do the following tasks. Tick the correct answer (true/false). Cite the passage of the text that proves your answer. Write down the line numbers and the first and last three words of your quotation. If the quote is less than six words, write down the full quote.

1. The British people were rather dissatisfied with politics so they voted to leave the EU. true / false

   line(s) _____ : _____

2. Most people who think immigrants should live a long time in Britain before they are entitled to welfare benefits voted Leave. true / false

   line(s) _____ : _____

3. The vote for Brexit shows the worries of a specific group of voters about certain consequences of EU membership. true / false

   line(s) _____ : _____

4. For those who voted Leave, the vote was about social class. true / false

   line(s) _____ : _____

5. Many politicians claim the Brexit vote was about sovereignty and other things. the EU. true / false

   line(s) _____ : _____

Total: ____ /5 VP

Part B: Analysis

Christo Kormanitski, 29 January 2013

ASSIGNMENT

Analyse the cartoon against the backdrop of the given text.

Part A: Comprehension – Solutions

ASSIGNMENTS

Read the text and do the following tasks. Tick the correct answer (true/false). Cite the passage of the text that proves your answer. Write down the line numbers and the first and last three words of your quotation. If the quote is less than six words, write down the full quote.

1. The British people were rather dissatisfied with politics so they voted to leave the EU.
   true ☐ false ☒

   line(s): 1–2: Britain's vote to … dissatisfaction with politics

2. Most people who think immigrants should live a long time in Britain before they are entitled to welfare benefits voted Leave.
   true ☒ false ☐

   line(s): 12–13: the longer any … leave the EU

3. The vote for Brexit shows the worries of a specific group of voters about certain consequences of EU membership.
   true ☒ false ☐

   line(s): 21–23: the outcome of … of EU membership

4. For those who voted Leave, the vote was about social class.
   true ☐ false ☒

   line(s): 25–26: "For leave voters, … consequences of it.

5. Many politicians claim the Brexit vote was about sovereignty and other things.
   true ☒ false ☐

   line(s): 41–42: Many politicians have … and other things

41

Part B: Analysis – Solutions

ASSIGNMENT

Cartoon:

I. Description:

background:
- clear sky with white clouds
- hilly landscape with grazing sheep

centre:
- a brick wall with a gate
- the wooden beams of the gate form a structure that looks like the Union jack
- it says "Great Britain" on the gate
- behind the gate there is a sheep dog which does not look very aggressive
- the dog is wearing a collar with metal spikes

foreground:
- two more sheep are trying to get into the pasture
- on their sides it says "Romania" and "Bulgaria"
- the two sheep are looking hopefully at the sheep dog
- they want to graze on the meadow like the sheep in the background
- the sheep dog is looking at them in a disinterested or neutral way
- the sheep dog and the closed gate prevent the two sheep from getting into the pasture

II. Interpretation:
- the grazing sheep in the background are foreign workers who are eating the grass of the pasture
- the pasture represents the British economy
- the grazing sheep stand for foreign workers who live off the British economy; they take jobs, earn money and draw benefits
- the gate and the sheep dog represent the British borders which will be closed to workers from the EU after Brexit
- the two sheep in front of the gate represent workers form poor member states of the EU who are trying in vain to get into Britain

III. Text:
- the Brexit vote was the result of anti-immigration feelings among the British public
- millions of people have come to Britain under the EU's freedom of movement rules in recent years
- those who voted Leave think that migrants should live for a long time in Britain before they can qualify for welfare benefits
- young, educated people were less negative about migration than older, uneducated people
→ Leave voters were concerned with immigration and its social consequences (i. e. migrants take jobs that would otherwise go to British people; migrants are entitled to benefits which cost the state a lot of money)

> **Topic:** Shaken, Not Stirred?! – The UK Between Tradition and Modernity
>
> **Skills:** Comprehension of a non-fictional text (newspaper article) (10 points); mediation (radio interview) (25 points)
>
> **Part A: Comprehension:** Royal Reform: The Royal Family Must Modernise in Order to Endure, The Times, 2015 (565 words)
>
> **Part B: Mediation:** 65. Thronjubiläum der Queen – Die einzig intakte Institution, Deutschlandfunk, 2017 (630 words)

Part A: Comprehension

Royal Reform: The Royal Family Must Modernise in Order to Endure

It is 14 years since the Duke of York[1] left the navy, and four since he stood down as the UK's special representative for international trade and investment. Since 1996 he has been unmarried. He is now under intense pressure to respond personally and forcefully to allegations[2] that in 2001 he had sex with a 17-year-old girl procured[3] for money and his amusement by a friend.

Whatever the veracity[4] of these claims, it is clear that while Prince Andrew's life out of uniform has not been short of entertainment, it has been short of structure. He has been content to craft for himself the portfolio[5] existence of a freelance[6] royal.

He has depended too much on his friends to help to support a lifestyle that, even as a scion[7] of one of Britain's richest families, he could not fund himself. And he has chosen those friends poorly.

As a result he is caught up in a scandal that will infuriate the Queen because of its potential to tarnish[8] not merely his own reputation but that of the royal family, so painstakingly[9] restored over the past two decades.

In the early 1990s the Queen acted decisively after what she called her annus horribilis[10] to end the perception of a royal family gallivanting[11] at public expense. She promised to pay income tax. Time was called[12] on the civil list[13]. Plans were drawn up to decommission[14] the Royal Yacht Britannia at considerable personal anguish for herself.

A series of lawyers' claims on behalf of a woman identified as Virginia Roberts do not yet constitute a crisis of confidence for the royals. Even so, a decisive response is needed. Put bluntly[15], the royal family, as an institution, is too big.

Too many of its members have official roles or spend time seeking them for want of[16] conventional occupations. For the sake of the family, and for the country, it should be streamlined.

As elected leaders wrestle with tight budgets and taxpayers struggle to fund them, it is only right that the royal family cuts its cloth[17] accordingly. This is not only a question of funds, but of expectations and an evolving[18] sense of what the monarchy stands for.

It has endured as a symbol of constancy and as a ceremonial focal point at times of national mourning and celebration. To go on enduring it must become more like the royal families that co-exist comfortably with modernity elsewhere in Europe, and less like the retrograde[19] clichés foisted[20] on it by an endlessly fascinated media.

---

[1] **the Duke of York Prince Andrew** (* 1960) the 2nd son and 3rd child of the Queen – [2] **allegation** (*fml.*) *Beschuldigung* – [3] **to procure** (*fml.*) to get a prostitute for sb. else to have sex with – [4] **veracity** (*fml.*) truth – [5] **portfolio** (*BE*) a particular area of responsibility, esp. of a government minister – [6] **freelance** *freiberuflich* – [7] **scion** [ˈsaɪən] (*lit.*) a young member of a rich and famous family – [8] **to tarnish** *beflecken* – [9] **painstaking** involving great care and effort – [10] **annus horribilis** [ˌænəs həˈrɪbɪlɪs] (*Lat.*) a horrible year filled with extremely bad events – [11] **to gallivant** (*infml.*) to go from one place to another looking for fun and entertainment without worrying about other things you should be doing – [12] **to call time** (*BE, idiom*) to decide to end sth. – [13] **the civil list** a sum of money granted by British Parliament each year to help the British royal family cover expenses; officially abolished in 2011 – [14] **to decommission** here: to take a ship out of active use – [15] **blunt** *unverblümt* – [16] **for want of sth.** because of a lack of sth. – [17] **to cut your coat** according to your cloth (*idm.*) to do only what you have enough money to do and no more – [18] **to evolve** to change – [19] **retrograde** (*fml., disappr.*) making a situation worse or returning to how sth. was in the past – [20] **to foist sth. on sb.** to force sb. to accept sth. they do not want

The monarchy's official duties should be performed by the Queen and those in direct line to
succeed her. Their siblings and cousins have often set inspiring examples. The Princess Royal's[21]
role as Olympic competitor and ambassador, Prince Harry's service in Afghanistan and his uncle Andrew's in the Falklands[22] come to mind. [...]

Britain's royal family has 18 official members, according to its website. Sweden's and Belgium's
have nine, Denmark's seven and Norway's five, all keeping official numbers low by making
clear distinctions between those with representative duties and those without.

The House of Windsor needs more clarity among these lines. More importantly, it needs a
clearer vision of itself, not as a crisis-prone[23] family business but as a family led by the head
of state. Last year Spain's king abdicated; this year his daughter could face trial for fraud[24]. No
royal family is indispensable[25], or permanent.

The Times, 7 January 2015

ASSIGNMENTS

Read the text and do the following tasks. Cite the passage of the text that proves your answer. Write down the line numbers and the first and last three words of the quotation. If the quote is less than six words, write down the full quote.

1. Tick the correct statement. ____/1 VP

Since Prince Andrew has left the navy he …

☐ … hasn't been able to cover all his daily expenses.

☐ … has fallen out with the royal family.

☐ … hasn't received any regular income as a member of the royal family.

☐ … has surrounded himself with friends who cared about nothing but his money.

line(s) _____ : _____

_____

2. Tick the correct answers (true/false). ____/4 VP

a) In the past, the Queen has made an effort to handle public money responsibly.   true ☐ false ☐

line(s) _____ : _____

_____

b) In view of the accusations brought against Prince Andrew, the royal family has again lost the public's trust.   true ☐ false ☐

line(s) _____ : _____

_____

c) Facing a new scandal with her son Andrew, the Queen feels obliged to react.   true ☐ false ☐

line(s) _____ : _____

_____

[21] **Princess Royal Anne** (*1950) the only daughter of the Queen – [22] **the Falklands** British Overseas Territory; reference to the Falklands War (April to June 1982) – [23] **crisis-prone** krisenanfällig – [24] **fraud** Betrug – [25] **indispensable** unverzichtbar

d) The royal family is made up of too many people.   true   false
                                                                               ☐   ☐

line(s) _____ : _____
_____

3. Tick the three correct statements.   ____/3 VP

According to the author of the text the British monarchy should …

☐ … follow the example of other royal families in Europe.

☐ … meet the media's expectations.

☐ … remain a symbol of stability.

☐ … reduce the number of members carrying out official duties.

☐ … stop relying on public money.

line(s) _____ : _____
_____

line(s) _____ : _____
_____

line(s) _____ : _____
_____

4. Tick the correct answers (true/false).   ____/2 VP

a) The author accuses the media of creating an outdated image of the monarchy.

line(s) _____ : _____
_____

b) The author wants to abolish the British monarchy altogether.   true   false
                                                                   ☐   ☐

line(s) _____ : _____
_____

                                                              Total: ____/10 VP

Part B: Mediation

65. Thronjubiläum der Queen – „Die einzig intakte Institution"

Benedikt Schulz: Das am längsten regierende Staatsoberhaupt der Welt steht vor dem nächsten Jubiläum. In wenigen Tagen feiert Elizabeth II ihr 65. Thronjubiläum, nachdem sie im vergangenen Jahr bereits ihren 90. Geburtstag gefeiert hat, unter großer Anteilnahme der britischen Bevölkerung. ... Und man kann sich des Eindrucks nicht erwehren, sie ist beliebter denn je. Über die Queen und die ungebrochene Bewunderung, die die Briten ihr zukommen lassen, habe ich gesprochen mit Thomas Kielinger, langjähriger Korrespondent in London der „Welt" und Autor einer Biographie der Queen. Ich habe ihn gefragt: Glauben Sie, dass sich die Queen zu ihren 65. Thronjubiläum vielleicht ein anderes Geschenk erhofft hat, als den Austritt ihres Landes aus der EU?

Thomas Kielinger: ... Die Königin ist bekanntlich sehr vorsichtig mit Äußerungen zu politischen Aktualitäten. Das ist auch einer der Gründe, warum sie so lange so populär geblieben ist. Sie will sich nicht mit irgendeiner Seite identifizieren, damit sie für alle Staatsoberhaupt[1] bleiben kann. Aber sie war nie besonders nah gegenüber Brüssel. Sie hat nur einmal die EU-Zentrale in Brüssel besucht. Es war nicht sehr folgenreich. Und dass der europäische Gerichtshof Souveränität über das englische Recht beansprucht, war bestimmt nicht in ihrem Sinne, so dass sie diese Brexit Entwicklung sehr gelassen entgegen geht. Sie ist der Souverän[2] eines unabhängigen Nationalstaates, und plötzlich, siehe da, kehrt England ein bisschen in den Status eines maritimen Nationalstaates zurück. Und ich glaube, damit macht sie ihren Frieden. Sie ist unsicher, wie es ausgehen mag, aber sie ist innerlich ganz gelassen bei diesem Vorgang.

Benedikt Schulz: Jetzt sind 65 Jahre ein großer Zeithorizont – wie hat sich die britische Gesellschaft seitdem verändert?

Thomas Kielinger: ... Die Veränderungen kamen in mehreren Schüben, und darum ist es sehr schwer, diese 65 Jahre Amtszeit auf einen Nenner zu bringen, anders als bei der großen Vorgängerin mit dem gleichen Namen, Elizabeth I. Da konnte man von einem goldenen Zeitalter sprechen – der Renaissance. ... Das war Kontinuität an der Staatsspitze wie jetzt, aber es war mehr eine Einheit. Eine Einheit der englischen Gesellschaft kann man wohl nicht behaupten unter der jetzigen Königin, es sei denn, ihre Dauer an der Spitze ist diese Klammer. Dies ist in der Tat auch die Ähnlichkeit mit Elizabeth I. Die Langlebigkeit an der Thronspitze, was die erste Elizabeth so gern mit dem lateinischen „Semper eadem", immer das Gleiche, das war das Lieblingsmotto der ersten Elizabeth. Das ist auch das Motto der jetzigen Königin. Innerhalb des Wandels immer die Gleiche: „The same procedure as every year." – wenn Sie so wollen. Und während man die Gesellschaft nicht auf einen Nenner bringen könnte in diesem Jahrzehnt des Wandels, ist die Königin ihr Hort der Stabilität und der Kontinuität.

Benedikt Schulz: Würden Sie denn sagen, dass die Königin die einzige stabile Kontinuität in einer Gesellschaft ist, die sich fortwährend wandelt und wo auch der Zusammenhalt brüchig wird?

Thomas Kielinger: Ja, das ist höflich ausgedrückt. Der Zusammenhalt ist jetzt gefährdet. England ist noch sehr unsicher, ob diese Entscheidung mit dem Brexit richtig war. Und dann haben wir ein zusätzliches Stichwort: Stabilität der Institutionen. Es gibt sehr viele Brüchigkeiten[3] heute: die Banken sind in der Bredouille seit der Krise, die politische Klasse genießt kein hohes Ansehen. Das gleiche gilt für die Medien. Und siehe da, diese Institution, die man vor 25 Jahren glaubte beendet zu sehen, nach dem Tod der Prinzessin Diana, und die Windsor Familie schien am Ende mit all ihren Skandalen. 25 Jahre später ist sie in der Tat die einzig intakte Institution. Und die Briten sind dankbar, dass sie diese Institution behalten haben und nicht vor 25 Jahren auf das Altengleis schoben. Die Queen ist lang genug am Leben, um alles erlebt zu haben: Höhen und Tiefpunkte. Aber sie vertritt eine Institution, die für die Briten ein Stück Beruhigung in der jetzigen Zeit ausmacht. ...

http://www.deutschlandfunk.de/65-thronjubilaeum-der-queen-die-einzig-intakte-institution.694.de.html?dram:article_id=377569, interview by Benedikt Schulz, 29 January 2017 [13.03.2017], transcribed by Katharina Einhoff

[1] **Staatsoberhaupt** head of state – [2] **Souverän** sovereign – [3] **Brüchigkeit** inconsistency

ASSIGNMENT

Your British friend has to give a presentation on the Queen and the British monarchy during the era of Brexit. Imagine you are listening to the interview "65. Thronjubiläum der Queen" on the radio. Write a letter to your friend summarizing what Kielinger says about the Queen's stance on Brexit and about the monarchy's role before and after the Brexit referendum. At the end of your letter, briefly state what you think the Queen's most important role is in our times.

Part A: Comprehension – Solutions

ASSIGNMENTS

1. Tick the correct statement.

Since Prince Andrew has left the navy he …

☒ … hasn't been able to cover all his expenses.

☐ … has fallen out with the royal family.

☐ … hasn't received any regular income as a member of the royal family.

☐ … has surrounded himself with friends who cared about nothing but his money.

line(s): 6–10 …, it is clear … not fund himself.

2. Tick the correct answers (true/false).

a) In the past, the Queen has made an effort to handle public money responsibly. — true ☒ false ☐
line(s) 14–15: In the early … at public expense.

b) In view of the accusations brought against Prince Andrew, the royal family has again lost the public's trust. — true ☐ false ☒
line(s) 18–19: A series of … for the royals.

c) Facing a new scandal with her son Andrew, the Queen feels obliged to react. — true ☐ false ☒
line(s) 19: Even so, a decisive response is needed.

d) The royal family is made up of too many people. — true ☒ false ☐
line(s) 33–35: Britain's royal family … and those without.

3. Tick the three correct statements.

According to the author of the text the British monarchy should …

☒ … follow the example of other royal families in Europe.

☐ … meet the media's expectations.

☒ … remain a symbol of stability.

☒ … reduce the number of members carrying out official duties.

☐ … stop relying on public money.

line(s) 26–27: To go on … elsewhere in Europe, …

line(s) 25–28: It has endured … endlessly fascinated media.

line(s) 29–30: The monarchy's official … to succeed her.

4. Tick the correct answers (true/false).

a) The author accuses the media of creating an outdated image of the monarchy.
line(s) 27–28: …, and less like … endlessly fascinated media.

b) The author wants to abolish the British monarchy altogether. — true ☐ false ☒
line(s) 36–38: …, it needs a … head of state.

Part B: Mediation – Solutions

ASSIGNMENT

Students are expected
- to generally respect the rules of mediation, i. e. the content and the language of the text should be in accordance with the text form (a letter), the addressee (a British friend) as well as cultural aspects (a German writing to a British friend) and situational aspects (a private situation).
- to mention why they are writing the letter, i. e. knowing that their British friend has to do a presentation on the Queen and the British monarchy in the era of Brexit and having listened to the interview on German radio, they offer to provide some additional information on the topic from the German point of view.
- to summarize what Kielinger said about the Queen's stance on Brexit, i. e.
  - the Queen doesn't want to identify with any position, she wants to be the head of state of all British people.
  - she has never shown any great affinity with or interest in the European Union and its institutions.
  - and doesn't seem to mind or really care if Great Britain actually leaves the EU.
- to sum up what Kielinger said about her and the monarchy's role before and after the Brexit referendum, i. e.
  - her motto being "Semper eadem" (always the same) she acts as the unifying force for a British society which is made up of different classes and cultures and which is above all deeply divided on Brexit.
  - the monarchy provides a functioning institution in contrast to other traditional institutions such as the political establishment, the financial system and the media, which are undergoing fundamental changes and facing uncertainties.
  - in summary, the monarchy stands for unity, stability and continuity in uncertain and unstable times.
- to comment on the Queen's most important role in our times.
  They may state that even in modern times the Queen is needed for the following reasons:
  - She stands for stability and continuity and is a unifying force (see Kielinger).
  - She is a symbol of Great Britain.
  - She acts as a role model e. g. when supporting charities.
  - She attracts tourists and thereby contributes to Great Britain's economy.

  They may also conclude that the Queen is unnecessary, citing the following reasons:
  - The monarchy is outdated and doesn't comply with the principles of democracy.
  - She doesn't have any real power.
  - The monarchy costs the taxpayers a lot of money.
  - The royal family is too scandal-ridden.

Topic: The American Dream – Reveries and Realities

Skills: Comprehension of a fictional text (screenplay) (5 points); mediation (newspaper article) (25 points)

Part A: Comprehension: Danny Strong: The Butler, 2013 (574 words)

Part B: Mediation: Frank Herrmann: Die wütenden Staaten von Amerika, 2014 (370 words)

Part A: Comprehension

Danny Strong

The Butler

EXT. WHITE HOUSE – GATE – DAY – 1968

HIPPIE PROTESTERS are outside the White House protesting the Vietnam War[1]. We hear their enraged chants:

5 HIPPIE PROTESTERS
HEY HEY LBJ[2], HOW MANY KIDS DID YOU KILL TODAY?! HEY HEY LBJ, HOW MANY KIDS DID YOU KILL TODAY?!

INT. WHITE HOUSE – RED ROOM – DAY –
10 1968

A maid cleans a mirror as she hears the chanting:

HIPPIE PROTESTERS V.O.[3]
HEY HEY, LBJ, HOW MANY KIDS DID YOU
15 KILL TODAY?!

MAID
I wish they'd shut up.

CUT TO – FULL SCREEN ARCHIVAL FOOTAGE – VIETNAM

20 American bombs drop on the JUNGLES of Vietnam.

INT. LORRAINE MOTEL[4] – MEMPHIS – DAY – 1968

MARTIN LUTHER KING, 38, wise, but weary[5], stands in the doorway, various AIDES
25 and STUDENTS fill the hotel room. Louis sits across from him. They are watching footage[6] of the Vietnam War on television.

NEWSCAST
30 "US casualties[7] are on the rise in Vietnam, giving fuel to critics who say there is no end in sight for what has become a bloody war."

Martin Luther King shakes his head, frustrated.

35 MARTIN LUTHER KING
President Johnson is making a tragic error in Vietnam.

LOUIS
Why shouldn't we fight in Vietnam?

40 MARTIN LUTHER KING
The Vietcong[8] don't call us niggers, for one.

Louis and a few aides laugh.

MARTIN LUTHER KING (CONT'D)
Seriously, how many of your parents support
45 this war?

Almost all raise their hands.

MARTIN LUTHER KING (CONT'D)
Well my Lord … (to Louis) Why do your parents support this?

50 LOUIS
We haven't spoken about it specifically, I just know they do.

MARTIN LUTHER KING
What do your daddy do?

55 Louis looks at him embarrassed.

---

[1] **Vietnam War** (1955–1975) a Cold-War era proxy-war (*Stellvertreterkrieg*) that took place in Vietnam, Laos and Cambodia and claimed the lives of more than one million people – [2] **LBJ** (*abbr.*) Lyndon B. Johnson, 36th President of the United States (1963–1969) – [3] **V.O.** (*abbr.*) voice over; used in a screenplay when the speaker is not shown in the shot – [4] **Lorraine Motel** name of the motel where Martin Luther King was assassinated on 4 April 1968 – [5] **weary** [ˈwɪəri] tired – [6] **footage** a piece of film, esp. showing a news event – [7] **casualty** a person injured or killed in a war – [8] **Vietcong** a South Vietnamese Communist front that fought a guerilla war against anti-communist forces – [9] **domestic** household servant – [10] **to defy** [dɪˈfaɪ] to refuse to obey sb./sth.

LOUIS
He's a butler.

MARTIN LUTHER KING
The black domestic[9] plays an important role in our history.

LOUIS
I didn't tell you that to make fun of me.

MARTIN LUTHER KING
Young brother, the black domestic defies[10] racial stereotypes by being hardworking and trustworthy. He slowly breaks down racial hatred with the example of his strong work ethic and dignified character.
(Then)
Now while we perceive the butler or the maid as being subservient[11], in many ways they are subversive[12] without even knowing it.

Louis stares at him, never thought about his dad in this way.

INT. BLAIR HOUSE[13] – R.D. WARNER'S OFFICE – DAY – 1968

Cecil sits across from the Chief Usher[14], R.D. Warner. Cecil is nervous, gripping his sweaty palms.

R.D. WARNER
Come in, Cecil.

CECIL
Good afternoon, Mr. Warner. Thank you for seeing me.

R.D. WARNER
What do you want?

CECIL
Since the colored … the black staff … does just as much work as the white staff, I believe that our salary should reflect our service, sir.

R.D. WARNER
'Black' staff?

CECIL
I also feel that we should have opportunities of advancement[15]. No black houseman has ever been promoted to the engineer's office.

R.D. Warner stares at Cecil for a long beat. Then –

R.D. WARNER
You're very well liked here, Cecil, but if you're unhappy with your salary or position, then I suggest you seek employment elsewhere.

CECIL
With all due respect sir …

R.D. WARNER
Don't let that Martin Luther King shit fill your britches[16] out. Just remember where I found you.

CECIL
Yes sir.

Long beat.

CECIL
Excuse me.

He walks out of the room, humiliated[17].

EXT. LORRAINE MOTEL – MEMPHIS
Martin Luther King stands on the balcony of the Lorraine Motel smoking a cigarette. We hear a newscast in V.O.:

TV NEWSCAST V.O.
Martin Luther King was shot and killed in Memphis today …

Danny Strong, The Butler, 2013, www.pages.drexel.edu/~ina22/splaylib/Screenplay-Butler.pdf [04.04.2015], pp. 71 ff.

Note: The 2013 historical drama film The Butler is based on the real-life experiences of Eugene Allen (1926 – 2010), an African American born on a cotton plantation in Georgia, who worked his way up from being a hotel servant to serving as a White House butler from 1952 to 1986. In the film version, the butler, Cecil Gaines, has a wife (Gloria) and two sons (Louis and Charlie). Louis, the older son, is a student who is actively involved in the Civil Rights Movement.

[11] **subservient** [səbˈsɜːviənt] *unterwürfig* – [12] **subversive** (*fml.*) *zersetzerisch* – [13] **Blair House** in Washington D.C. is the official state guest house for the President of the United States – [14] **Chief Usher** the person who manages the entire service staff in the White House – [15] **advancement** the development or improvement of sth.; here: better job opportunities – [16] **too big for your britches** (*AmE, infml., idiom*) with too high an opinion of yourself – [17] **humiliated** *erniedrigt*

ASSIGNMENTS

Read the text and do the following tasks. If required, cite the passage of the text that proves your answer. Write down the line numbers and the first and last three words of the quotation. If the quote is less than six words, write down the full quote.

1. Tick the correct statement. ____/1 VP

Apart from the hippies, the following person thinks that the U.S. should stop the war in Vietnam:

☐ a maid working at the White House

☐ Louis

☐ Louis' father

☐ Martin Luther King

line(s) _____ : _____

_____

2. Tick the correct statement. ____/1 VP

Louis …

☐ … discusses politics with his parents at home.

☐ … first takes offense at Martin Luther King's observations about his father's job.

☐ … has adopted his parents' view on the Vietnam War.

☐ … is proud of his father working as a butler at the White House.

line(s) _____ : _____

_____

3. Complete the following sentences. ____/2 VP

a) Reflecting on what Martin Luther King has said about the position and function of black domestics, Louis realizes that _____

_____

b) According to Martin Luther King, Louis' father contributes to changing the image of African Americans because _____

_____

4. Tick the correct statement. ____/1 VP

When Cecil asks for a pay raise, R.D. Warner …

☐ … shows understanding for Cecil's request.

☐ … offers him a new job.

☐ … appreciates the contribution of the black staff.

☐ … voices his disapproval of the Civil Rights Movement.

line(s) _____ : _____

_____

Total: ____/5 VP

Part B: Mediation

Frank Herrmann

Die wütenden Staaten von Amerika

Washington. Schießwütig[1] und rassistisch: So denken nicht nur Schwarze über Amerikas Polizisten. Die Entscheidungen in New York und Missouri, Beamte[2] nicht für ihr tödliches Handeln zu bestrafen, untergraben[3] das Vertrauen in den Rechtsstaat. Im ganzen Land demonstrieren Tausende.

Es ist ein Sit-in im Neonlichtermeer, zwischen den häuserwandgroßen Reklametafeln am Times Square. „I can't breathe, I can't breathe", skandieren die Demonstranten, während sie tapfer ausharren in der Nachtkälte. „Ich kriege keine Luft mehr": Das waren die letzten aufgezeichneten Worte von Eric Garner. Der schwarze New Yorker starb im Juli auf dem Weg ins Krankenhaus, nachdem ihn Polizisten in den Schwitzkasten[4] genommen und seinen Kopf rabiat aufs Pflaster eines Bürgersteigs gedrückt hatten.

Garner war 43 Jahre alt und Vater von sechs Kindern. Er hatte vor einem Laden auf Staten Island Zigaretten verkauft; lose, nicht in Packungen, woraufhin ihn eine Streife wegen illegaler Geschäfte festnehmen wollte. Er litt an Asthma und einem schwachen Herzen. Während er den Beamten, die ihn umzingelten, im Ton der Verzweiflung zurief, sie sollten ihn endlich in Ruhe lassen, wurde er von hinten zu Boden gerissen. Auf dem Video einer Handykamera, aufgezeichnet von einem Freund Garners, kann man die Szene lückenlos sehen. Die Aufnahmen lassen keinen Zweifel daran, dass es die Polizisten waren, die einen Mann angriffen, der keinerlei Bedrohung darstellte.

Schon das unterscheidet den Tod Eric Garners vom Tod Michael Browns, des Jugendlichen, der in der US-Kleinstadt Ferguson erschossen wurde. Während Brown den Ordnungshüter, der ihn nach einem Ladendiebstahl anzuhalten versuchte, wütend mit Fausthieben attackierte, flehte Garner nur, dass man ihn nicht anrühren solle. Doch genau wie im Fall Browns entschied eine Grand Jury, besetzt mit 14 weißen und neun nichtweißen Geschworenen, niemanden vor einen Richter zu stellen. Auch nicht Daniel Pantaleo, der Garner in den Schwitzkasten nahm, obwohl solche Griffe nach den Bestimmungen des New York Police Department verboten sind.

Wie klar oder knapp die Jury eine Anklage[5] am Mittwoch ablehnte, bleibt vorläufig unter Verschluss[6]. Das Gremium tagte im Geheimen, so wie im November in Ferguson auch. Doch im Unterschied zu der heruntergekommenen Kleinstadt in Missouri, wo nach dem Urteil reihenweise Geschäfte in Flammen aufgingen, scheinen die Weltbürger der Millionenmetropole gerade jetzt ihre Toleranz unter Beweis stellen zu wollen: die Demonstranten zeigten ihre Wut, blieben aber friedlich.

(370 words)

www.rp-online.de/politik/ausland/new-york-city-die-wuetenden-staaten-von-amerika-aid-1.4717605, 5 December 2014 [02.04.2015]

ASSIGNMENTS

After watching the film *The Butler*, you come across the article *Die wütenden Staaten von Amerika*. Both deal with racism in the U.S. – the film referring to the past and the article to the present. You feel intrigued and want to share your thoughts and feelings about racism in the U.S. with your American friend.

Write an e-mail to your American friend in which you report the main facts given in the article *Die wütenden Staaten von Amerika*. You explain how the article reminds you of the film, referring to the scenes described in the screenplay excerpt presented in Part A. Finally, tell your friend what you think about racism in the U.S.

[1]**schießwütig** trigger-happy – [2]**Beamter** civil servant – [3]**untergraben** to undermine – [4]**jdn. in den Schwitzkasten nehmen** to get/hold sb. in a headlock – [5]**Anklage (erheben)** (to press) charges against sb. – [6]**unter Verschluss bleiben** to remain classified

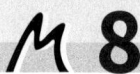

Part A: Comprehension – Solutions

ASSIGNMENTS

1. **Tick the correct statement.**

   Apart from the hippies, the following person thinks that the US should stop the war in Vietnam:

   ☐ a maid working at the White House

   ☐ Louis

   ☐ Louis' father

   ☒ Martin Luther King

   line(s) 36 – 37: President Johnson is … error in Vietnam.

2. **Tick the correct statement.**

   Louis …

   ☐ … discusses politics with his parents at home.

   ☒ … first takes offense at Martin Luther King's observations about his father's job.

   ☐ … has adopted his parents' view on the Vietnam War.

   ☐ … is proud of his father working as a butler at the White House.

   line(s) 51: I didn't tell … fun of me.

3. **Complete the following sentences.**

   a) Reflecting on what Martin Luther King has said about the position and function of black domestics, Louis realizes that **he had never thought about his dad in that way./black domestics are being subversive.**

   b) According to Martin Luther King, Louis' father contributes to changing the image of African Americans because **he slowly breaks down racial prejudices with the example of his strong work ethic and dignified character.**

4. **Tick the correct statement.**

   When Cecil asks for a pay raise, R.D. Warner …

   ☐ … shows understanding for Cecil's request.

   ☐ … offers him a new job.

   ☐ … appreciates the contribution of the black staff.

   ☒ … voices his disapproval of the Civil Rights Movement.

   line(s) 102 – 104: Don't let that … your britches out.

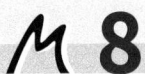

Part B: Mediation – Solutions

ASSIGNMENT

Students are expected

- to generally respect the rules of mediation, i. e. the content and the language of the text should be in accordance with the text form (an e-mail), the addressee (an American friend) as well as cultural aspects (a German writing to an American) and situational aspects (private, informal communication between friends).
- to mention why they are writing the e-mail, i. e. they have watched the film *The Butler* and read the article *Die wütenden Staaten von Amerika* and want to share their thoughts and feelings with their American friend about racism in the U.S.
- to report on the main facts given in the article. According to the article
  - protests are taking place across the U.S. as a consequence of growing police brutality towards African Americans. The article reports on the killing of two African Americans by the police, the youngster Michael Brown who was shot when the police tried to arrest him for robbery and Eric Garner who died when the police arrested him for illegally selling cigarettes in front of a store on Long Island and kept him in a headlock even though he was telling the police officers that he couldn't breathe.
  - in contrast to Brown who fought back with his fists, Garner didn't show any resistance and only begged not to be touched.
  - a friend of Garner recorded the whole incident on his mobile.
  - in both cases the Grand Jury consisting of 14 white and 9 non-white jurors decided not to press charges against the police officers.
  - the demonstrations in New York remained peaceful in contrast to the reactions in Ferguson, which were more violent and aggressive.
- to explain how the article relates to the film.
  - In both the article as well as the film scenes, African Americans are treated unfairly. The butler Cecil isn't paid as much as his white colleagues and he doesn't stand a chance of getting a promotion. When he asks for equal treatment, he is scoffed at by his employer in a humiliating way. Michael Brown and Eric Garner are likewise treated in a disproportionally brutal way. The article as well as the film scenes reveal the flagrant racist attitude of whites towards African Americans in the past and present.
- to comment on racism in the U.S. by e. g.
  - voicing their surprise or even shock at these blatant acts of racism.
  - expressing their worry about a phenomenon which was thought to have been overcome, but is obviously still present.
  - siding with the people peacefully protesting against the unfair treatment of African Americans, pointing out that anybody experiencing racism needs society's solidarity.
  - reflecting upon what could be done to overcome racial prejudices.
  - comparing the situation in the U.S. with the situation in Germany, for example by referring to refugees and other immigrants who are victims of racist abuse and attacks.

> **Topic:** Child Labour in India
>
> **Skills:** Comprehension of a non-fictional text (online article) (5 points); Mediation of a text (25 points)
>
> **Part A: Comprehension:** Josh Jacobs, Reeva Misra: Child Labor: The Inconvenient Truth Behind India's Growth Story (online article/blog; 614 words) (5 points)
>
> **Part B: Mediation:** SOS Kinderdörfer weltweit: Kinderarbeit in Indien

Part A: Comprehension

Josh Jacobs, Reeva Misra

Child Labor: The Inconvenient Truth Behind India's Growth Story

Seventy years ago last week, India gained independence. The country has since created one of the world's largest economies. But despite its wealth, 33 million children from ages 5 to 18 are working – and almost one third of this group are under 15 according to *Save the Children India*, making India home to one of the highest concentrations of child workers in the world.

5 Economic theory suggests that child labor would be all but eradicated[1] by growth and development. But after some successful efforts to increase the number of children in school and to rehabilitate former child workers, the national effort to eliminate the practice is losing momentum[2] and child labor in major cities has increased significantly, according to interviews with more than a dozen child rights groups, academics and international organizations. […]

10 But the nation's development has been segmented[3], and much of it has not impacted[4] the areas of the economy where children tend to work. "India's GDP[5] and growth is largely oriented around a highly educated and highly skilled workforce," said Rajeev Dehejia, professor of public policy at New York University. "This is paradoxical for an economy where most people have a low level of education."

15 Conversely, most child labor is concentrated away from the skilled economy, in the informal sector that makes up about 90 percent of India's workforce and half of its GDP, according to Credit Suisse[6] estimates. Here, children are not subject to government inspections, legal protections or minimum wage requirements. Such industries include agriculture, small factories for carpets and clothing, brick kilns[7] and domestic staffing.

20 "It is very under the table," said Nina Smith, chief executive of *GoodWeave International*, which works against child labor in global supply chains. "There is a huge workforce that is unregulated, does not really benefit from labor laws, and is highly vulnerable to exploitation."

The Indian government says that there has been a decline of 45 percent between 2005 and 2010. But most child rights groups give a more conservative estimate, as government figures do not 25 include all children or all parts of the informal economy.

Some suggest that child labor rates have plateaued[8] in the years since the last census, but with no new national count and the definition of child labor constantly changing, the exact number is unknown. It is a challenge to generate precise figures because of the covert[9] nature of the practice; many children are kept in hidden workplaces, such as employers' homes and small-30 scale factories.

Puja Marwaha, chief executive of *Child Rights and You*, a major Indian nongovernmental organization, said that child labor has redistributed as children have migrated to large cities like Mumbai and Delhi in search of work. To bolster[10] her case, she cites government data showing a 60 percent increase in the number of children working in Mumbai in the decade leading up to 35 the most recent census in 2011. […]

---

[1] **to eradicate** to abolish completely – [2] **to lose momentum** to become weaker or slower – [3] **segmented** divided into separate parts – [4] **to impact** to influence – [5] **GDP** Gross Domestic Product – [6] **Credit Suisse** Swiss bank – [7] **brick kiln** *Ziegelei* – [8] **to plateau** to stay on the same level – [9] **covert** hidden, secret – [10] **to bolster** to support

Many development economists think that eradicating child labor boosts long-term growth, by increasing wages (children tend to be paid less, which depresses average wages) and by creating a more skilled economy.

"There is vast literature showing that child labor impedes[11] development," said Sandra Polaski,
40 who worked on child labor reforms for India as deputy director-general of the *International Labor Organization* from 2012 to 2016. "It certainly impedes the development of the individuals affected, but it also impedes the development of the overall economy, because your future workforce is going to be less well educated."

It also takes jobs from elsewhere in the economy. UNICEF this year calculated global unem-
45 ployment would be reduced by 200 million, if the world's 160 million children aged 5 to 14 who are working were sent to school instead. [...]

The Washington Post Wonkblog, 21 August 2017
https://www.washingtonpost.com/news/wonk/wp/2017/08/21/child-labor-the-inconvenient-truth-behind-indias-growth-story/?utm-term=961f2c0ac50b [10.03.2018]

ASSIGNMENTS

Read the text and do the following tasks. If required, cite the passage of the text that proves your answer. Write down the line numbers and the first and last three words of the quotation. If the quote is less than six words, write down the full quote.

1. Tick the correct answer (true/false). ____/1 VP

According to one theory, a booming economy leads to a decrease in the number of children working.

true ☐ false ☐

line(s) _____ : _____

_____

2. Tick the correct statement.

Children working in the so-called informal sector … ____/1 VP

☐ … are inspected by the government, protected by lawyers and do not earn any money.

☐ … do not undergo government inspections, are not protected by law and not entitled to a minimum wage.

☐ … must undergo government inspections, are protected by law and are entitled to a minimum wage.

☐ … are not subjects of the Indian government and cannot fight for adequate payment with the help of a lawyer.

line(s) _____ : _____

_____

3. Tick the correct answer (true/false). ____/1 VP

It is difficult to say how many children work because child labour usually does not take place in the open.

true ☐ false ☐

line(s) _____ : _____

_____

[11] **to impede** to prevent

4. Write the correct letters in the boxes below. ____/2 VP

Match the statements about child labour in India to the person who said them (Rajeev Dehejia, Nina Smith, Puja Marwaha or Sandra Polaski).

Note: Two of the statements are not found in the text.

A very many workers have no rights and are potentially exploited

B child labour does not help development

C parents should be held responsible if they do not provide adequate education for their children

D India's economic growth is due to highly skilled and educated workers

E there should be a legal reform to make education compulsory

F child labour is now found in cities like Mumbai and Delhi

Rajeev Dehejia	
Nina Smith	
Puja Marwaha	
Sandra Polaski	

Total: ____/5 VP

Part B: Mediation

Kinderarbeit in Indien

Fakten zu wirtschaftlichen Ausbeutung von Kindern

Welche Ursachen für Kinderarbeit in Indien gibt es?
Trotz des Wirtschaftsbooms in Indien in den vergangenen Jahren leben immer noch mehr als ein Drittel aller Inder unter der Armutsgrenze. Denn die technischen Innovationen und Weiterentwicklungen im IT-Bereich haben keine Arbeitsplätze in den Armutsgebieten geschaffen. Menschen aus ländlichen Gebieten mit wenig Bildung sehen häufig keine andere Möglichkeit, als ihre Kinder aus den Schulen zu nehmen und arbeiten zu lassen, um die Familien zu ernähren. Aus Not werden Kinder von ihren Vätern und Müttern auch an Kinderhändler verkauft. Oder die Eltern lassen ihre Kinder auf dem Land zurück, um in einer Großstadt Arbeit zu suchen – und die Kinder sind auf sich allein gestellt. Nicht selten geraten auch sie dann in die Fänge von Kinderhändlern, die die Jungen und Mädchen für einen sehr geringen oder gar keinen Lohn arbeiten lassen.

Welche Gesetze gegen Kinderarbeit gibt es?
Zwar wurde von der indischen Regierung bereits 1993 ein Gesetz gegen Kinderarbeit in Indien erlassen, das gefährliche Arbeiten oder Tätigkeiten, die die geistige, seelische, sittliche oder soziale Entwicklung von Mädchen und Jungen unter 18 Jahren schädigen könnten, verbietet – aber stoppen konnte es die Ausbeutung von Kindern nicht. Denn das Gesetz hat viele Schlupflöcher. Beispielsweise erlaubt es die Mitarbeit der Kinder im elterlichen Betrieb. So wird das Drehen von Zigarillos schnell zur Vollzeitbeschäftigung nicht nur der Eltern, sondern auch der Kinder.
Zudem bekleiden zahlreiche Unternehmer wie zum Beispiel Minenbesitzer ein politisches Amt – und den Firmenbossen ist nicht daran gelegen, die billigen Kinderarbeiter aus ihren Unternehmen zu verbannen.
In den Jahren 2006 sowie 2016 wurde das Gesetz gegen Kinderarbeit noch verschärft: Seitdem ist auch die Arbeit als Haushaltshilfen oder Servicepersonal in Restaurants und Hotels für Kinder unter 14 Jahren verboten. Die Arbeit in Familienbetrieben bleibt aber weiterhin ungeahndet. Zudem gilt das Gesetz nicht für 15- bis 17-Jährige, denen lediglich die Verrichtung „gefährlicher" Arbeiten verboten ist. Davon werden allerdings Tätigkeiten wie Feldarbeit, bei der die Minderjährigen massiv Pestiziden ausgesetzt werden, oder körperlich anstrengendes Teppichweben nicht ausgeschlossen.
Damit diese Vorschrift auch in der Praxis beachtet wird, diskutiert die indische Regierung momentan über ein weiteres Gesetz, das den Einsatz von Kindern unter 14 Jahren als Arbeitskräfte mit einer mehrjährigen Gefängnisstrafe ahndet anstatt lediglich mit Geldstrafen.

Wie kann man Kinderarbeit in Indien stoppen?
In der Politik muss sich noch viel mehr tun: Die Gesetze gegen Kinderarbeit müssen in Indien weiter verschärft und vor allem strikt angewendet werden. Darüber hinaus gilt es, extreme Armut nachhaltig zu bekämpfen. Nur so lässt sich in Indien die Kinderarbeit stoppen. Ein Hauptziel muss dabei immer auch sein, dass Kinder zur Schule gehen können, statt arbeiten zu müssen. Denn durch Bildung lässt sich der Teufelskreis aus Armut und Kinderarbeit durchbrechen. Wenn Kinder eine bessere Schulbildung erhalten, finden sie als Erwachsene leichter eine anständig bezahlte Arbeit und können mit ihrem Einkommen für sich und ihre Familie sorgen – ohne auf die Mithilfe der Kinder angewiesen zu sein. Zwar besteht in Indien bereits eine Schulpflicht bis zum 14. Lebensjahr und die Teilnahme am Unterricht ist kostenlos. Aber aufgrund der Armut der Familien gilt meist die Devise: Etwas zu Essen zu haben ist wichtiger als Bildung. Daher besuchen viele Kinder die Schule nur unregelmäßig, weil sie stattdessen arbeiten müssen.

SOS Kinderdörfer weltweit, https://www.sos-kinderdörfer.de/unsere-arbeit/wo-wir-helfen/asien/indien/kinderarbeit-in-indien [10.03.2018]

ASSIGNMENTS

You are taking part in an international symposium on child labour and are writing a report (in English) on child labour in India. Summarize the situation of working children in India and what can be done to improve their situation. Use the information given in the English and German texts.

Part A: Comprehension – Solutions

ASSIGNMENTS

1. Tick the correct answer (true/false).

According to one theory, a booming economy leads to a decrease in the number of children working. — true ☒ false ☐

line(s) 5 – 6: Economic theory suggests … growth and development.

2. Tick the correct statement.

Children working in the so-called informal sector …

☒ … do not undergo government inspections, are not protected by law and not entitled to a minimum wage.

line(s) 17 – 18: Here, children are … minimum wage requirements.

3. Tick the correct answer (true/false).

It is difficult to say how many children work because child labour usually does not take place in the open. — true ☒ false ☐

line(s) 28 – 29: It is a … of the practice

4. Write the correct letters in the boxes below.

Match the statements about child labour in India to the person who said them (Rajeev Dehejia, Nina Smith, Puja Marwaha or Sandra Polaski).

Note: Two of the statements are not found in the text.

Rajeev Dehejia	D
Nina Smith	A
Puja Marwaha	F
Sandra Polaski	B

Part B: Mediation – Solutions

ASSIGNMENT

India is one of the fastest growing economies in the world but still 33 million children between the ages 5 and 18 work, and almost one third of this group are under the age of 15.

What are the reasons for this paradox?

The financial situation of many families is so bad that children have to support their families financially, which means these children cannot go to school and acquire an education. Some children are even sold by their parents to people they have to work for. Sometimes parents leave their children in the country and move to big cities to get jobs there. The children have to take care of themselves.

Children work in the so-called informal sector of the economy that includes areas like agriculture, small factories for carpets and clothing, brick kilns, hotels, restaurants or private homes. This sector is not controlled by the government, so there is no legal protection for these children and nobody makes sure that they are paid a minimum wage. Many children are even hidden in the factories where they work or in their employers' houses. This makes it difficult to determine how many children exactly work, but there has been a trend of working children moving away from the country and into large cities like Mumbai or Delhi.

There is legislation which officially bans child labour. A law which was passed in 1993 bans children under the age of 18 from working in dangerous jobs which inhibit their mental, ethical or social development, but children are still exploited as they are officially allowed to work in their parents' businesses. Even stricter laws were made in 2006 and 2016. Since then it has been forbidden for children under the age of 14 to work in households, restaurants or hotels but they still can work in family businesses. Children between the ages of 15 and 17 are only forbidden to do "dangerous work". But they can work, for example, in the agricultural sector where they are exposed to massive amounts of pesticides, or in carpet factories where work is very exhausting.

The question now is what can be done to help children in India?

First, stricter laws have to be passed and, even more importantly, the government has to make sure these are really enforced. Then the extreme poverty in some parts of Indian society has to be fought. This means that children have to be free to go to school and get an education, for only education can break through the vicious circle of poverty and child labour: When children are better educated they will find good jobs more easily. And so they will earn more money and be able to sustain their families without the help of their children.

Topic: History of Britain in the European Union

Skills: Comprehension of a non-fictional text (online article) (5 points); analysis of a text (25 points)

Part A: Comprehension: Dr Daniel Kenealy: How Did We Get Here? A Brief History of Britain's Membership of the EU (blog post, 604 words)

Part B: Mediation: Jens-Peter Marquardt: Großbritannien und Europa: Schon immer ein bisschen außen vor (online article, 387 words)

Part A: Comprehension

Dr Daniel Kenealy

How Did We Get Here? A Brief History of Britain's Membership of the EU

The Long Term: Britain as an Awkward European Partner?
In the aftermath of World War II, the US took a strategic foreign policy decision to underwrite[1] the security of Western Europe. It did this as a result of an altered balance of power. Put simply, the war transformed Europe from the centre of global politics to a component in a new balance of power between the US and the Soviet Union.

Within Europe, France decided, in the early 1950s, to make a bold[2] move. Foreign Minister Robert Schuman proposed a new institution: the European Coal and Steel Community (ECSC), which would place the coal and steel industries of Germany, France and several other European countries under international control.

The aim was to take what were then considered industries essential[3] to warfare and place them beyond the control of any one country. The underpinning[4] idea was to make it less likely that any major European country could ever wage war[5] against another.

Whilst Italy, Belgium, the Netherlands, and Luxembourg were content to join the ECSC, the UK opted[6] to stay out. Within the British government, a combination of facts came together to determine that outcome. In elite circles, there was a strong belief that Britain remained, after World War II, a global power of the first rank, a status that would be compromised[7] by joining new European institutions.

This sense was coupled with a belief that Britain's rightful role was to serve as a bridge between Europe and the US, and Europe and the Commonwealth, a role that it could only play if it stood aside from European integration. In addition, given that the ECSC did not permit the nationalisation of its members' coal and steel industries, and that the post-war Labour Government was committed to such nationalisation, it would have been politically difficult for Britain to join.

Britain thus stood on the sidelines as six European countries took the first step towards integration. A few years later, between 1955–1957, those same six countries decided to establish the European Economic Community (EEC), which was a commitment to create a single market in which goods, services, people, and capital moved feely.

This was the start of what today we call the European Union. It was driven by a desire to boost trade and economic growth. Once again, Britain stood aside in 1957, driven largely by an understanding of its role in the world that did not allow it to tie its fortunes too closely to the Continent.

Knocking on the Door
By the early 1960s Britain's economic growth and foreign direct investment were disappointing compared to the EEC six. As it became clear that we were lagging behind[8] our Continental neighbours, the government changed tack[9] and attempted to join them.

Governments led by both parties – Harold Macmillan's Conservatives and Harold Wilson's Labour – tried in vain to secure membership throughout the 1960s. The obstacle was French Presi-

---

[1] **to underwrite** to guarantee – [2] **bold** kühn – [3] **essential** very important – [4] **underpinning** supporting – [5] **to wage war** to begin a war – [6] **to opt** to choose – [7] **to compromise** to put in danger, to put at risk – [8] **to lag behind** to remain behind – [9] **to change tack** to change the approach or direction, *das Ruder herumreißen*

dent Charles De Gaulle who, in an attempt to further his geopolitical aim of French leadership of a larger European bloc in global politics, twice said "Non" to British membership in 1961 and 1967. Eventually Britain's persistent knocking on the door of the EEC paid off. De Gaulle had departed the scene and, with the European balance of power shifting clearly and decisively in favour
40 of West Germany, French
President Georges Pompidou lifted his country's opposition to British membership.
Membership was secured on 1 January 1973 under the Conservative government of Edward Heath. But Heath lost power the following year and in 1975, shortly after joining, Britain held its first Europe referendum to decide whether or not it should stay in the EEC. [...]

Scotland's academic blog on Europe, from the University of Edinburgh; European Futures, 24 May 2016
http://www.europeanfutures.ed.ac.uk/article-3278 [10.03.2018]

ASSIGNMENTS

Read the text and do the following tasks. If required, cite the passage of the text that proves your answer. Write down the line numbers and the first and last three words of the quotation. If the quote is less than six words, write down the full quote.

1. **Tick the correct statement. (true/false)**

   After the Second World War, Europe no longer played a central role but became part of a new system dominated by the USA and the Soviet Union.   true false

   line(s) _____ : _____

   _____

2. **Tick the correct statement.**

   The underlying aim of the ECSC was …

   ☐ … to make another European war less likely.

   ☐ … to put the steel industries of the member states under international control.

   ☐ … to strengthen the steel industries of the member states on the international steel market.

   ☐ … to unite the steel industries of Germany, France, and several other European countries.

   line(s) _____ : _____

   _____

3. **Tick the correct statement. (true/false)**

   The UK did not join the ECSC because some parts of British society were afraid it would be too expensive.   true false

   line(s) _____ : _____

   _____

4. **Complete the sentence. You may use your own words or quote from the text.**

   In 1957 Britain did not join the EEC because _____

   _____

5. **Complete the sentence. You may use your own words or quote from the text.**

   French president Charles de Gaulle did not want Britain to join the EEC because _____

   _____

   Total: ____ /5 VP

Part B: Mediation

Jens-Peter Marquardt

Großbritannien und Europa: Schon immer ein bisschen außen vor

Bereits nach dem Ende des Zweiten Weltkrieges begaben sich die Briten freiwillig in eine Außenseiterposition. Zur Montanunion traten sie nicht bei und auch die Römischen Verträge unterzeichneten sie nicht. Dass sie nun aus der EU austreten, wirkt vor diesem Hintergrund wenig überraschend.

19. September 1946: Europa lag noch in Trümmern, als Winston Churchill[1] einer Einladung an die Universität Zürich folgte und dort seine Vision von der Zukunft Europas vorstellte. [...]
Churchills Idee der Vereinigten Staaten von Europa war damals revolutionär. Doch für sein eigenes Land hatte der Sieger des zweiten Weltkrieges darin keinen Platz vorgesehen. Zunächst lief auch alles nach Churchills Plan. Der Kontinent mit Franzosen und Deutschen an der Spitze, machte sich auf, ein neues Europa zu schaffen, und die Briten schauten zu.

Als die Montanunion gegründet wurde, ließ die britische Regierung die Frist fürs Mitmachen verstreichen: Der Premierminister war gerade nicht in London, der Außenminister war im Krankenhaus, der Finanzminister lag krank zu Hause – das Restkabinett sah sich nicht in der Lage, eine Entscheidung für den Beitritt zur Montanunion zu treffen.

Zu den Verhandlungen über die Gründung der EWG schickte die Britische Regierung dann ledglich einen untergeordneten Handelsgesandten, der weder dort, noch in London ernst genommen wurde. Als sechs europäische Länder 1957 schließlich die Römischen Verträge unterschrieben, war Großbritannien nicht dabei. [...]

Fehler der Zurückhaltung

Auch die Briten erkannten schon wenige Jahre nach der Unterzeichnung der Römischen Verträge, dass sie einen Fehler gemacht hatten. Der damalige Premierminister Harold Macmillan realisierte, wie schnell sich der europäische Kontinent durch den Wegfall der Handelsschranken von den Kriegsfolgen erholte, Großbritannien aber zurückblieb und die Deutschen den Wirtschaftsaufschwung dominierten. [...]

Neue Chance für die Briten

Die Briten bekamen erst eine neue Chance, als de Gaulle abtrat, George Pompidou in den Elysee-Palast einzog und Edward Heath in London Premierminister wurde. Großbritannien wurde 1973 Mitglied der EWG.

„Wir waren wirtschaftlich damals immer noch der kranke Mann Europas. Das Argument, zu einer Gemeinschaft zu gehören, der es wirtschaftlich gut ging, war stärker als das Verlangen nach größerer nationaler Souveränität," sagt der frühere britische Außenminister William Hague.

Doch nicht alle überzeugte dieses Argument. Ein Teil der britischen Konservativen hat die Zugehörigkeit zur EWG und später zur EU nie akzeptiert. Am 23. Juni vergangenen Jahres waren sie endlich am Ziel: Die britischen Bürger stimmten beim EU-Referendum mit 52 zu 48 Prozent für den Austritt.

http://www.deutschlandfunk.de/grossbritannien-udn-europa-schon-immer-ein-bisschen-aussen.795.de.htm?dram:article_id=381654 [10.03.2018]

ASSIGNMENTS

A British friend is preparing a presentation on the history of Britain's membership in the EU. He has found the following German text on the Internet and thinks it might be a good idea to include the point of view of a German journalist in his presentation. However, he doesn't speak German well enough to fully understand it. So he asks you for help. Mediate the text above.

[1] **Winston Churchill** British conservative politician and prime minister from 1940 to 1945 and from 1951 to 1955

Part A: Comprehension – Solutions

ASSIGNMENTS

Read the text and do the following tasks. If required, cite the passage of the text that proves your answer. Write down the line numbers and the first and last three words of the quotation. If the quote is less than six words, write down the full quote.

1. the correct statement. (true/false)

After the Second World War, Europe no longer played a central role but became part of a new system dominated by the USA and the Soviet Union.

true ☒   false ☐

line(s): 4 – 5: the war transformed … the Soviet Union.

2. Tick the correct statement.

The underlying aim of the ECSC was …

☒ … to make another European war less likely.

☐ … to put the steel industries of the member states under international control.

☐ … to strengthen the steel industries of the member states on the international steel market.

☐ … to unite the steel industries of Germany, France, and several other European countries.

line(s): 11 – 12: The underpinning idea … war against another.

3. Tick the correct statement. (true/false)

The UK did not join the ECSC because some parts of British society were afraid it would be too expensive.

true ☐   false ☒

line(s): 15 – 17: In elite circles … new European institutions.

4. Complete the sentence. You may use your own words or quote from the text.

In 1957 Britain did not join the EEC because <u>Britain saw itself as an international power and therefore did not want to link itself too closely to the European countries on the continent</u>.

5. Complete the sentence. You may use your own words or quote from the text.

French president Charles de Gaulle did not want Britain to join the EEC because <u>he wanted France to have a leading role in a European bloc in international politics</u>.

Part B: Mediation – Solutions

ASSIGNMENTS

Jens-Peter Marquardt argues that Great Britain adopted the role of an outsider of the EU from the very beginning as it neither joined the ECSC nor ratified the Treaty of Rome. So for Marquardt it is not surprising that Britain is going to leave the EU.

To explain Britain's hesitant attitude towards the EU and its predecessors, Marquardt goes back as far as 1946, when, shortly after the Second World War, Winston Churchill explained his revolutionary vision of Europe in a speech at the University of Zurich.

First, things went as he had planned: continental Europe under the leadership of Germany and France began to flourish while Great Britain, one of the winners of the war, stayed on the sidelines.

The next two steps on the path to a united Europe, the foundation of the ECSC and the ratification of the Treaty of Rome, did not seem to be important enough for the British government to become actively involved.

However, shortly after the ratification of the Treaty of Rome the British realized that it had been a mistake not to take the EEC seriously as the Continent recovered from the war far more quickly than Britain and Germany dominated the economic boom.

When French president Charles de Gaulle resigned from office, Great Britain finally became a member of the EEC in 1973.

Former British foreign secretary William Hague said that in those days it was more important for Britain to belong to an economically successful organization than to be a completely sovereign state independent of the rules and regulations of such an organization.

The author of the text, Jens-Peter Marquardt, thinks that a part of the British conservatives were never convinced of this argument and they had finally reached their aim on 23 June 2016, when 52 percent of the British citizens voted Leave and only 48 percent voted Remain.

© Westermann Gruppe, Best.-Nr. 040187

Topic: The World Going Global

Skills: Comprehension of a non-fictional text (comment/blog post) (5 points); composition (25 points)

Part A: Comprehension: Mike Kercheval: Why Online Retailers Continue to Open Brick-and-Mortar Stores (471 words)

Part B: Composition: Describe and interpret the visual: Caritas: "Far away is closer than you think"

Part A: Comprehension

Mike Kercheval

Why Online Retailers[1] Continue to Open Brick-and-Mortar Stores[2]

In an age when new technology and the growth of pure online-only retailers[1] have industry analysts questioning the future of brick-and-mortar[2] stores, what are online retailers doing to grow their businesses and gain market share? Why, opening up physical[3] storefronts of course. The benefits that physical spaces provide make up three of the top reasons why online retailers are setting up shops, including: multisensory[4] consumer experiences, better logistics and consumer service offerings and strong, lasting brand relationships.

The rise of omni-channel retail strategies[5] in which mobile, online and in-store experiences complement[6], rather than compete with, one another has ushered[7] in a new era for online retailers. Birchbox and Frank & Oak are just a couple of examples of e-tailers[8] that have planted roots to remain competitive and provide a seamless[9] customer experience across all shopping channels.

And it's no wonder they're buying up real estate[10]; the economics speak for themselves. According to our latest consumer survey, 78 percent of consumers prefer to shop in-store and they spend six times more in-store than online. This is reflected in the fact that the majority of all retail sales still occur in the physical store. In 2013, the U.S. Census Bureau reported that 94 percent of retail sales were conducted[11] in brick-and-mortar stores, while just 6 percent occurred online. Physical stores are simply good business.

Multisensory Consumer Experiences
Nothing beats holding a product in your hand, feeling the fabric[12] and seeing the minute[13] details – something that can't be done online. We found that 73 percent of consumers want to try on or touch merchandise before they make a purchase. Physical shopping centers allow consumers to do just this — interact with a range of products to make informed decisions about what they're buying.

Furthermore, physical stores have been busy retrofitting[14] their spaces with technological advancements that make the in-store customer experience more efficient, which effectively eliminates the guessing games encountered online. Is the size or fabric not quite right? Or maybe it fits perfectly, but you want to try on every color option available? These are solvable problems when you are shopping in a physical store. [...]

Just this month, Amazon.com announced it is opening a physical storefront in the middle of New York City, the first of its kind in the company's 20-year history as an online retailing giant. The store will be located in Herald Square, near the famous Macy's department store and

---

[1] **retailer** a business that sells goods to the public – [2] **brick-and-mortar** store a traditional shop that is located in a real building – [3] **physical** here: real and able to be seen and touched – [4] **multisensory** able to be experienced by more than one of the physical senses of touch, smell, taste, hearing, and sight – [5] **omni-channel** retail strategy system of using many different distribution methods to sell products – [6] **complement** *ergänzen* – [7] **to usher (in)** to lead the way, introduce – [8] **e-tailer** (*abbr.*) electronic retailer; a business selling products online – [9] **seamless** smooth and without difficulties – [10] **real estate** [ˈrɪəl ɪˌsteɪt] land and/or buildings – [11] **to conduct an activity** *etw. durchführen* – [12] **fabric** *Faser, Gewebe* – [13] **minute** [maɪˈnjuːt] extremely small – [14] **to retrofit** *nachrüsten*

67

the Empire State Building, an area that receives some of the most significant foot traffic[15] in the city. This announcement speaks to[16] the importance of an omni-channel strategy, and certainly could have significant positive effects on the real estate side of the retailing business. [...]
This is why online retailers are looking to the physical store as an avenue[17] to meaningfully en-
45 gage customers and build strong, trusted and lasting relationships.

http://techcrunch.com/2014/10/31/why-online-retailers-continue-to-open-brick-and-mortar-stores, 31 October 2014 [03.04.2015]

ASSIGNMENTS

Read the text and do the following tasks. If required, cite the passage of the text that proves your answer. Write down the line numbers and the first and last three words of the quotation. If the quote is less than six words, write down the full quote.

1. **Tick the correct answers (true/false).** ____/3 VP

    a) Against all expectations, online retailers are launching brick-and-mortar stores.　true　false

    line(s) _____ : _____

    _____

    b) Brick-and-mortar retailers are gradually replacing Internet-based retailers.　true　false

    line(s) _____ : _____

    _____

    c) Numerous statistics have proven that off-line shopping is more attractive than online shopping.　true　false

    line(s) _____ : _____

    _____

2. **Complete the following sentences.** ____/2 VP

    a) In-store shopping allows customers to check on _____

    _____

    b) According to the text, retailers ultimately aim to _____

    _____

    Total: ____/5 VP

---

[15] **foot traffic** *Fußgängerverkehr* – [16] **to speak to sth.** (*phr.v.*) to signal, show – [17] **avenue** here: a way of achieving sth.

Part B: Composition

Caritas: Far Away Is Closer Than You Think

ASSIGNMENT

Describe and interpret the visual. What can be done to ensure that the benefits of globalization are more equally shared? Comment.

Part A: Comprehension – Solutions

ASSIGNMENTS

1. **Tick the correct answers (true/false).**

   a) Against all expectations, online retailers are launching brick-and-mortar stores.
   line(s) 1–3: In an age … storefronts of course.
   true ☒ false ☐

   b) Brick-and-mortar retailers are gradually replacing Internet-based retailers.
   line(s) 7–8: The rise of omni-channel … for online retailers.
   true ☐ **false** ☒

   c) Numerous statistics have proven that off-line shopping is more attractive than online shopping.
   line(s) 11–16: According to our … percent occurred online.
   true ☒ false ☐

2. **Complete the following sentences.**

   a) In-store shopping allows customers to check **the size, fabric, colour and other details of the product.**

   b) According to the text, retailers ultimately aim to **meaningfully engage customers and build strong, trusted and lasting relationships with them.**

Part B: Composition – Solutions

ASSIGNMENT

Students are expected

- to write a short introduction mentioning
    - the type of visual (a picture, an advertisement)
    - the title ("Far away is closer than you think")
    - the general topic (e. g. consequences of globalization, the gap between industrial and developing countries, globalization and the fashion industry)
    - the date of publication (2014 as part of a campaign led by Caritas Germany)
    - the source (accessed via the Internet on 11 August 2017)
- to describe the picture, referring to
    - the division of the picture into two parts: one part, the left half of the picture, depicts a delighted woman in a modern shop looking for and buying clothes and shoes in the sales rack; the other part, the right half of the picture, shows miserable workers in a sweatshop sewing the clothes the woman in the other part is buying. The two parts are separated by a wall and linked by a clothing rack.
    - the atmosphere, which is light and friendly in the shop and heavy and depressing in the sweatshop.
    - the stark contrast between the two parts of the picture, which is emphasized by the use of bright and warm colours in the left half and the use of dull and dark colours in the right half of the picture.
    - the text situated in the bottom right-hand corner of the picture.
- to analyse the picture, i. e. they should
    - mention the phenomenon of globalization and briefly explain it.
    - describe the consequences of globalization on the fashion industry, i. e. outsourcing of the production of clothes to developing countries, extremely low-priced clothes in developed countries at the expense of the people producing the clothes in the developing countries in unbearable working conditions, i. e. long working hours, low salaries, dangerous workplaces, generally inhumane treatment of workers.
    - point out that globalization has not benefited everybody equally, that some people and nations are actually profiting more than others.
    - mention that with the campaign "Far away is closer than you think" by Caritas Germany is trying to raise awareness of the fact that in our globalized world everything is connected and that our actions have consequences for people far away, i. e. in developing countries. The aim of this advertisement is to make people reflect upon and rethink their consumer practices.
- to present and evaluate different ways of making sure that the benefits of globalization are more equally shared, they should e. g.
    - point out possible measures to be taken, e. g. setting up and implementing fair-trade standards and an inspection system to make sure that working conditions in developing countries are improved and workers' rights are protected; or from a consumer perspective: buying only fair-trade products.
    - evaluate the measures according to their feasibility and efficiency.

> **Topic:** The American Dream – Reveries and Realities
>
> **Skills:** Comprehension of a non-fictional text (newspaper article) (5 points); composition (25 points)
>
> **Part A: Comprehension:** Hank Sanders, Faya Rose Toure: Still Waiting in Selma (476 words)
>
> **Part B: Composition:** Write a letter to the editor

Part A: Comprehension

Hank Sanders, Faya Rose Toure

Still Waiting in Selma

On March 25, 1965, tens of thousands of us gathered before the Alabama State Capitol, the endpoint of a five-day, 54-mile march from Selma to Montgomery. Dr. Martin Luther King Jr. called out, "How long?" and the crowd responded, "Not long!" The moment was electric. We believed it would not be long before the right to vote was deeply rooted and bearing fruit[1] in America.

5 In one sense, we were right. The Voting Rights Act[2], passed just months after the Selma marches, banned the discriminatory voting practices[3] that many southern states had enacted following the Civil War. Over time, the Act enabled millions of African-Americans to register to vote, and for decades following its passage, voting rights continued to slowly expand. But in another sense we are still waiting. Either Dr. King was wrong or "not long" is biblical, measured in generations.

10 We came to Selma in 1971, newly married and fresh out of Harvard Law School. Our intentions were to stay for five years. We were sure that by then Dr. King's vision of voting rights would have been realized. Over 40 years later, not only are the fruits scarce[4], but the roots are shallow[5] and feeble[6].

Celebrations, commemorations[7] and movies make people feel good, but the reality is that vot-
15 ing rights have been rolled back dramatically in recent years. […] Today, all Alabama voters must show photo identification. In Alabama and other states, this I.D. must be government-issued[8]. These policies, which disproportionately affect minority, poor and elderly voters who are less likely to possess government-issued I.D.s, are the 21st-century equivalent of the Jim Crow-era poll tax[9] and literacy test.

20 Dr. King understood that voting would be the last right granted to African-Americans because it was the most powerful. Indeed, if we had better understood our history, we would not have been surprised that "not long" has stretched into a half-century. […]

But what of Selma, the worldwide symbol of voting rights and freedom?

As Dr. King urged[10], we marched on the ballot boxes[11]. In 1965 there were 300 registered Af-
25 rican-American voters and zero African-American elected officials in Dallas County, where Selma is located; in 2015 there were 19,862 registered African-American voters and 19 African-American elected officials. But we greatly underestimated the power of those who control the voting process. […]

Despite our city's fame as a cornerstone of the Civil Rights movement, African-Americans in
30 Selma who dare to discuss these issues openly and honestly are called racists, haters and worse. Yes, we marched on the ballot boxes. But for the tens of thousands of African-Americans in Selma, life, as Langston Hughes said, "ain't been no crystal stair." Better off is not equal.

We came to Selma over four decades ago; today we are both in our seventies. When we arrived, we agreed that every five years we would decide anew whether to stay or leave. Each time we

---

[1] **to bear fruit** (*fml.*) to produce successful results – [2] **Voting Rights Act of 1965** an act signed into law by President Lyndon B. Johnson that prohibited racial discrimination in voting – [3] **voting practices** a standard or accepted way of organizing the election process – [4] **scarce** not easy to find or get – [5] **shallow** [ˈʃæləʊ] not deep – [6] **feeble** weak and unstable – [7] **commemoration** [kəˌmeməˈreɪʃən] *Gedenkfeier, Gedenkveranstaltung* – [8] **government-issued** officially provided by the government – [9] **poll tax** here: money that had to be paid in order to be allowed vote – [10] **to urge** [ɜːdʒ] to strongly advise sb. to do sth. – [11] **ballot box** *Wahlurne*

chose to stay. The choice is coming up again next year. What shall we do? The struggle continues because the challenges remain great.

http://www.nytimes.com/2015/03/07/opinion/still-waiting-in-selma.html?_r=0,6 March 2015 [05.04.2015]

ASSIGNMENTS

Read the text and do the following tasks. Cite the passage of the text that proves your answer. Write down the line numbers and the first and last three words of the quotation. If the quote is less than six words, write down the full quote.

1. **Tick the correct statement.** _____/1 VP

   In Selma, African-Americans are still waiting for …

   ☐ … all barriers to equal voting rights to be removed.

   ☐ … public debates about race relations to be held.

   ☐ … the right to apply for photo I.D. cards.

   ☐ … the Voting Rights Act to be passed.

   line(s) _____ : _____

   _____

2. **Tick the correct answers (true/false).** _____/3 VP

   a) Thanks to the Voting Rights Act, there is no discrimination in elections today. true ☐ false ☐

   line(s) _____ : _____

   _____

   b) Gaining equal voting rights was one of Martin Luther King's key issues. true ☐ false ☐

   line(s) _____ : _____

   _____

   c) Selma is still a place for productive dialogue about African-Americans' civil rights. true ☐ false ☐

   line(s) _____ : _____

   _____

3. **Tick the correct statement.** _____/1 VP

   The authors of the text are

   ☐ confused

   ☐ frustrated

   ☐ hopeful

   ☐ shocked

   with regard to the current situation of African-Americans in Selma.

   line(s) _____ : _____

   _____

   Total: _____/5 VP

Part B: Composition

ASSIGNMENT

Write a letter to the editor in which you comment on the authors' observation that "[o]ver 40 years later, not only are the fruits scarce, but the roots are shallow and feeble" (ll. 13 f.). Take into consideration what you know about discrimination against African-American citizens in America today. Furthermore, give the authors some advice as to what they should do, thereby answering their question at the end of the article.

Part A: Comprehension – Solutions

ASSIGNMENTS

1. **Tick the correct statement.**

   In Selma, African-Americans are still waiting for all
   ☐ barriers to equal voting rights to be removed.
   ☒ public debates about race relations to be held.
   ☐ the right to apply for photo I.D. cards.
   ☐ the Voting Rights Act to be passed.

   line(s) 16 – 23: Today, all Alabama … into a half-century.

2. **Tick the correct answers (true/false).**

   a) Thanks to the Voting Rights Act, there is no discrimination in elections today. true ☐ false ☒

   line(s) 14 – 15: …, but the reality is … in recent years.

   b) Gaining equal voting rights was one of Martin Luther King's key issues. true ☒ false ☐

   line(s) 20 – 21: Dr. King understood that … the most powerful.

   c) Selma is still a place for productive dialogue about African-Americans' civil rights. true ☐ false ☒

   line(s) 29 – 30: Despite our city's … haters and worse.

3. **Tick the correct statement.**

   The authors of the text are
   ☐ confused
   ☒ frustrated
   ☐ hopeful
   ☐ shocked

   with regard to the current situation of African-Americans in Selma.

   line(s): 7 – 9 Over time, the … are still waiting.

   Or: line(s): 11 – 12 We were sure … are shallow and feeble.

Part B: Composition – Solutions

ASSIGNMENT

Students are expected

- to respect the rules of writing a letter to the editor, i. e.
    - to write the formulae used at the beginning and at the end of a letter
    - to clearly refer to the article
    - to comment on the authors' observations and answer their question at the end.
- to explain the authors' statement that despite all the efforts of the Civil Rights Movement and the following years to ensure that African-Americans are granted equal rights, they are still facing various forms of discrimination. They are frustrated that there have only been minor improvements ("… not only are the fruits scarce" l. 13) and that racism still lingers in the very heart of 21st-century society ("… the roots are shallow and feeble" ll. 13 – 14). According to the authors, this is seen in today's voting practices, which subtly discriminate against African-Americans.
- to point out that indeed racism has always been and, with Trump as the current president of the U.S., has become an even more controversial issue in American society, sparking recurring social unrest and racial tension.
- to point to the fact that the situation of African-Americans seems to have generally improved by referring to the example given by the authors ("… in 2015 there were 19,862 registered African-American voters and 19 African-American elected officials …" ll. 26 – 27) and by providing more examples, e. g.
    - the growing number of influential African-Americans (e. g. Barack Obama, Oprah Winfrey)
    - the growing number of successful African-American artists in the music and film industry (e. g. Beyoncé, the Oscar-winning film Moonlight with an all-black cast)
    - increased opportunities to move up the career ladder.
- to admit that racism still seems to be a social issue of paramount importance for various reasons, e. g.
    - the disproportionately high number of unemployed African-Americans living below the poverty line
    - the difference in income
    - the life expectancy of African-Americans which is generally lower than that of whites
    - the disproportionately high number of African-Americans being "stopped and frisked" by the police and being victims of police shootings (e. g. Trayvon Martin, 2012; Eric Garner, 2014; Michael Brown, 2014 to name only a few)
    - the growing number of white nationalist protests (e. g. Charlottesville).
- to draw a conclusion as to the current situation of African-Americans in the US, taking into account all the aspects mentioned and examples given, thereby either (partly) siding with the authors or (partly) disagreeing with them.
- to refer to the authors' question of whether they should leave Selma – a question they have raised every 5 years since they arrived in Selma – in view of the ongoing racial discrimination African-Americans are still facing today. Students can recommend leaving Selma, arguing for example that the few improvements that have been achieved for African-Americans are not enough and that they should seek a better life elsewhere where they will be treated more fairly. Or they can come to the conclusion that they should stay, arguing for example that some changes require a very long time and that they must not abandon the anti-racism cause.

Topic: Shaken, Not Stirred?! – The UK Between Tradition and Modernity

Skills: Comprehension of a non-fictional text (magazine article) (10 points); composition (25 points)

Part A: Comprehension: Ethnic Minorities: Breaking Out (468 words)

Part B: Composition: Comment on the integration process of immigrants.

Part A: Comprehension

Ethnic Minorities: Breaking Out

In Britain, Bangladeshis have overtaken Pakistanis. Credit[1] the poor job market when they arrived and the magical effect of London.

Fatima Patel, the editor of Asian Sunday, a local newspaper, says Bradford's leaders look ruefully[2] at Tower Hamlets, a poor borough[3] of London 200 miles to the south. And that comparison has an ethnic tinge[4], because Bradford is heavily Pakistani, whereas Tower Hamlets is the heart of Bangladeshi Britain.

In many people's minds, and often in official statistics, the 447,201 people who called themselves Bangladeshi in the 2011 census and the 1,124,511 who identified themselves as Pakistani are lumped[5] together. And the two groups have much in common. Mass immigration for both began in the 1950s. Both are largely working-class and Muslim. Both tend to vote Labour. Both are concentrated in one business – restaurants in the case of Bangladeshis, taxi-driving among Pakistanis. But their fortunes[6] are now diverging[7]. And that says something about what it takes to succeed as an immigrant in Britain. [...]

Bangladeshis born in Britain are [...] more likely than their Pakistani counterparts to socialise with people of a different ethnicity, according to [one] study. Both still overwhelmingly wed[8] within their own ethnic group. But among young men, for whom marrying out[9] is easier, 26 % of Bangladeshis now do so compared with 17 % of Pakistani youths. [...]

The growing success of Bangladeshis appears odd because their living conditions are often so dismal[10]. More than one-third live in social housing, compared with a national average of 18 %. Near Morpeth School, a fence outside grotty[11] flats is topped[12] with upturned nails to deter[13] intruders. Pakistanis are more likely to own houses. But, since those houses are often in the wrong place that has not helped them much. Those living in decayed[14] northern towns are tied to[15] properties whose value is hardly rising, stopping them moving to more dynamic spots. "It is a stake[16] that only allows you to move around the corner to equally bleak[17] economies," says Mr Saggar.

Cultural conservatism, which has deepened among many British Pakistanis, makes things worse. Cousin marriage is more common among Pakistanis than among Bangladeshis, as is the bringing over of partners from the subcontinent, argues Parveen Akhtar, a sociologist at the University of Bradford. Nuzhat Ali, a campaigner in the city, reckons[18] such marriages are actually more common among recent[19] Pakistani migrants than among their grandparents. The practice[20] means that more Pakistanis in a city like Bradford are first-generation migrants than might be expected by now. It might also mean that young men are less driven to succeed – the desire to find a marriage partner being an unstated[21] reason for going to university among people of all races.

The experience of Bangladeshis suggests that it is foolish to judge the success of immigrants after just a few years in Britain.

The Economist, 21 February 2015, pp. 29 f.

[1] **to credit sb./sth. with sth.** to say that sb./sth. is responsible for sth., especially something good – [2] **rueful** ['ruːfəl] (lit.) feeling sorry and full of regret – [3] **borough** ['bʌrə] part of a city with its own local government – [4] **tinge** [tɪndʒ] ein Hauch von etw. – [5] **to lump sb./sth. together** (phr.v.) etw./jdn. über einen Kamm scheren – [6] **fortune** Schicksal – [7] **to diverge** [ˌdaɪˈvɜːdʒ] to become different or follow a different direction – [8] **to wed** to marry sb. – [9] **to marry out** to marry sb. from a different culture – [10] **dismal** miserable, gloomy – [11] **grotty** (infml.) dirty, run-down – [12] **to top sth.** etw. überragen – [13] **to deter** [dɪˈtɜːr] abschrecken – [14] **decayed** heruntergekommen – [15] **to be tied to sth.** an etw. gebunden sein – [16] **stake** a wooden or metal post that is pushed into the ground and that sb./sth. is tied to – [17] **bleak** sad and without hope – [18] **to reckon** to think that sth. is probably true – [19] **recent** here: newly-arrived – [20] **practice** Brauch – [21] **unstated** implizit

ASSIGNMENTS

Read the text and do the following tasks. If required, cite the passage of the text that proves your answer. Write down the line numbers and the first and last three words of the quotation. If the quote is less than six words, write down the full quote.

1. Tick the correct statement. ___/1 VP

The text deals with …

☐ … immigration to Great Britain today.

☐ … the reasons why Bangladeshis are more integrated than Pakistanis.

☐ … the relationship between Bangladeshis and Pakistanis.

☐ … the welcome Bangladeshis and Pakistanis have received in Great Britain.

2. Match the ethnic groups with the actions and fill in the corresponding letters. One characteristic cannot be attributed to any of them. ___/6 VP

Bangladeshis	Pakistanis	Both

A. are currently moving to other regions   **B.** often live in poor-quality housing

C. are friends with people from other cultures   **D.** are more likely to own a house

E. prefer to choose a partner from their own community to start a family

F. are less open to adapting to British culture   **G.** tend to work in the service sector

3. Tick the correct answers (true/false). Cite the line(s) in the text that proves your answer. ___/2 VP

a) The British have always thought of both Bangladeshis and Pakistanis as people from the Indian subcontinent.   true ☐   false ☐

line(s) _____ : _____

_____

b) The number of first-generation immigrants from Pakistan has been decreasing with time.   true ☐   false ☐

line(s) _____ : _____

_____

4. Tick the correct statement. Cite the line(s) in the text that proves your answer. ___/1 VP

The conclusion the author draws is that …

☐ … Bangladeshis have found it as difficult as the Pakistanis to integrate.

☐ … Great Britain has to invest in the integration of Pakistanis.

☐ … immigration to Great Britain has increased in recent years.

☐ … only time will show whether immigrants ultimately achieve success in a country.

line(s) _____ : _____

_____

Total: ___/10 VP

Part B: Composition

ASSIGNMENT

In the concluding sentence, the author states that "it is foolish to judge the success of immigrants after just a few years in Britain" (ll. 34 – 35).
Comment on this statement, referring to aspects mentioned in the text as well as your knowledge of multicultural societies as discussed in class. Include ideas about what societies can do to facilitate the integration process.

Part A: Comprehension – Solutions

ASSIGNMENTS

1. Tick the correct statement.

The text deals with …

☐ … immigration to Great Britain today.

☒ … the reasons why Bangladeshis are more integrated than Pakistanis.

☐ … the relationship between Bangladeshis and Pakistanis.

☐ … the welcome Bangladeshis and Pakistanis have received in Great Britain.

2. Match the ethnic groups with the actions and fill in the corresponding letters. One characteristic cannot be attributed to any of them.

Bangladeshis	Pakistanis	Both
B, C	D, F	E, G

3. Tick the correct answers (true/false).

a) The British have always thought of both Bangladeshis and Pakistanis as people from the Indian subcontinent.   true ☒   false ☐

line(s) 7–9: In many people's … are lumped together.

b) The number of first-generation immigrants from Pakistan has been decreasing with time.   true ☐   false ☒

line(s) 29–31: The practice means … expected by now.

4. Tick the correct statement.

The conclusion the author draws is that …

☐ … Bangladeshis have found it as difficult as the Pakistanis to integrate.

☐ … Great Britain has to invest in the integration of Pakistanis.

☐ … immigration from the Indian subcontinent to Great Britain has increased in recent years.

☒ … only time will show whether immigrants ultimately achieve success in a country.

line(s) 34–35: The experience of … years in Britain.

Part B: Composition – Solutions

ASSIGNMENT

Students are expected

- to define what "success" generally means with regard to immigrants, e. g. being integrated into the society of the host country, speaking the local language, being able to earn a living, finding decent housing, socializing with natives, taking part in social activities in the host country.

- to describe the situation of Pakistanis and Bangladeshis as presented in the text.
  Both ethnic groups have much in common, e. g. they have lived in Britain since the 1950s, are largely working-class and Muslim, vote Labour, tend to work in the service sector, live under disadvantageous conditions – Bangladeshis are more likely to live in social housing, Pakistanis own houses in run-down areas which are difficult to sell.
  In contrast to Pakistanis who increasingly tend to isolate themselves, for example by marrying within their community (cousin marriage), Bangladeshis are more open to mixing with natives. Even though they generally marry within their community as well, the number of young Bangladeshis marrying out is higher than that of young Pakistanis.

- to explain the author's statement by referring to the situation of the two ethnic groups mentioned in the text.
  Even though both ethnic groups arrived in Britain at the same time and faced the same difficulties, Bangladeshis are considered to be more successful than Pakistanis – a fact that can be linked to their willingness to mingle more with natives, thereby showing a greater openness to the culture of their host country.

- to compare the situation of Pakistanis and Bangladeshis to the situation of immigrants in other multicultural societies.
  In general, it can be stated that isolation or exclusion of immigrants leads to more fear and distrust on both sides (immigrants and natives), making the successful integration of immigrants even more difficult.

- to point out more aspects which have made the integration of immigrants in Britain and in other countries more challenging, e. g. the globally increasing distrust of Muslims due to terrorist groups such as ISIS and Al Qaida, the growing number of young radicalized Muslims or increasingly restrictive immigration policies worldwide.

- to present ideas as to how to facilitate the integration of immigrants.
  - There is no doubt that in order to ensure that the integration of immigrants is successful an open and unbiased attitude is necessary and long-term efforts have to be made on both sides.
  - Host societies could for example offer integration or language courses and even oblige immigrants to attend them, recognize foreign qualifications, provide educational opportunities, facilitate access to the job market, develop and improve urban areas in order to prevent ghettos from developing.
  - Immigrants could for example make an effort to learn the language of their host country, socialize with native people, invest in their education, promote mixed schools, find a job, join clubs, get involved in their local community.
  - It is in any case a two-way process.

- to draw a conclusion referring to the author's statement that "it is foolish to judge the success of immigrants after just a few years in Britain." The integration process depends on various complex factors and sometimes takes many years or even generations to achieve successfully.

> **Topic:** English as a global language
>
> **Skills:** Comprehension of a non-fictional text (online article) (10 points); composition (25 points)
>
> **Part A: Comprehension:** Hephzibah Anderson, How Americanisms are Killing the English Language (674 words)
>
> **Part B: Composition:** Discuss whether the German language needs to be protected by the German Constitution.

Part A: Comprehension

Hephzibah Anderson

How Americanisms Are Killing the English Language

A book released this year claims that Americanisms will have completely absorbed the English language by 2120. Hephzibah Anderson takes a look.

So it turns out I can no longer speak English. This was the alarming realisation foisted[1] upon me by Matthew Engel's witty, cantankerous[2] yet nonetheless persuasive polemic[3] That's the Way It
5 Crumbles: The American Conquest of English. Because by English, I mean British English.
Despite having been born, raised and educated on British shores, it seems my mother tongue has been irreparably corrupted by the linguistic equivalent of the grey squirrel[4]. And I'm not alone. Whether you're a lover or a loather[5] of phrases like "Can I get a decaf soy latte to go?", chances are your vocabulary has been similarly colonised.
10 Speaking on the wireless[6] in 1935, Alistair Cooke declared that "Every Englishman listening to me now unconsciously uses 30 or 40 Americanisms a day". In 2017, that number is likely closer to three or four hundred, Engel hazards[7] – more for a teenager, "if they use that many words in a day".
But how did this happen and why should we care? After all, as a nation we've been both in-
15 vaded and invader, and our language is all the richer for it. Words like bungalow, bazaar, even Blighty[8], have their roots elsewhere. Heck, go far enough back and isn't it pretty much all just distorted Latin, French or German? […]
With no means of swift communication or easeful passage between the two countries, American English merely trickled[9] back into its source to begin with. But as the balance of power be-
20 tween Britain and her former colonies shifted, as America ascended to military, economic, cultural and technological dominance, that trickle swelled to a torrent[10], washing away any kind of quality control. […]
Nowadays, no sphere of expression remains untouched. Students talk of campus and semesters. […]
25 It's understandable, of course. Sometimes, American words just seem more glamorous. Who wants to live in a flat, a word redolent of damp problems and unidentifiable carpet stains, a word that just sounds – well, flat – when they could make their home in an apartment instead? […]
We've already reached the point where most of us can no longer tell whether a word is an Americanism or not. By 2120, [Engel] suggests, American English will have absorbed the Brit-
30 ish version entirely. As he puts it, "The child will have eaten its mother, but only because the mother insisted". […]
Even so, you might ask, is this really such a bad thing? When my grandfather returned home from the front in World War Two, he became a firm believer in the unifying powers of Espe-

---

[1] **to foist sth. upon sb.** to force sb. to accept sth. – [2] **cantankerous** bad-tempered and always complaining – [3] **polemic** here: a book conveying a strong message – [4] **grey squirrel** a species of squirrel from North America that was brought to Europe and has displaced the native red squirrel population in the UK – [5] **to loathe** to hate – [6] **on the wireless** on the radio – [7] **to hazard** to make a guess – [8] **Blighty** used in the First and Second World War by soldiers to refer to Great Britain or England – [9] **to trickle** to flow slowly and gradually – [10] **torrent** a large amount of water flowing very quickly

ranto. Along with Volapuk, Ekselsioro and Mondlingvo[11], that idealistic tongue came to nothing. American English is succeeding where it failed. But it's hard not to feel that diminishing linguistic variance isn't shrinking the world. [...]

And then there's the very valid theory that you can't feel or think things for which you've no language. A borrowed vocabulary, one that's evolved to meet the needs of people whose lives are subtly but profoundly different (ask anyone who's lived Stateside for a while – those superficial similarities and familiarities soon fall away to reveal a decidedly foreign country), deprives[12] us of fully experiencing our own. [...]

It might seem tactless to bemoan[13] the state of any branch of all-conquering English when so many other languages are being wiped out entirely. But ultimately, the battle isn't really one of British versus American English, but of individual experience versus the homogenising effects of global digital culture. For a provocative glimpse of where this might all lead, it's worth noting that Globish, a "sort-of language" (Engel's phrase) created for business types by former IBM exec Jean-Paul Nerriere, consists of just 1,500 words. Jokes, metaphors and acronyms are verboten, being too fraught[14] with potential for misunderstanding. Personally, I think I'd rather communicate in emojis. But here's hoping it won't come to that. Engel's book is certainly a wake-up call. Sorry, *cri de coeur*. Wait, better make that a call to arms.

http://www.bbc.co.uk/culture/story/20170904-how-americanisms-are-killing-the-english-language 4 September 2017 [07.10.2017]

ASSIGNMENTS

Read the text and do the following tasks. If required, cite the passage of the text that proves your answer. Write down the line numbers and the first and last three words of the quotation. If the quote is less than six words, write down the full quote.

1. Tick the correct answers (true/false). ____/3 VP

a) The author cannot speak English. true false

line(s) _____ : _____
_____

b) American words and expressions have been integrated not only into the author's language, but into other people's languages as well. true false

line(s) _____ : _____
_____

c) Americanisms can be more often found in the language of young people. true false

line(s) _____ : _____
_____

2. Tick the two correct statements. ____/2 VP

According to the author, the reasons for the growing number of Americanisms in British English are …

☐ … America's increasing power.

☐ … the simplicity of the American language.

[11]**Volapuk, Ekselsioro, Mondlingvo** artificial languages – [12]**to deprive sb. of sth.** to stop sb. from doing sth. – [13]**to bemoan** to complain about sth. – [14]**fraught** full of sth. unpleasant

☐ ... the indifference of the British people towards the changes their language is undergoing.

☐ ... the charm of American words and expressions.

☐ ... the flexibility of the English language.

line(s) _____ : _____

_____

line(s) _____ : _____

_____

3. Complete the following sentences using your own words or with words from the text. ____/2 VP

a) According to the author, Esperanto _____

_____

_____

b) A country's words and expressions cannot be replaced by those of another country because

_____

_____

_____

4. Tick the correct answers (true/false). ____/3 VP

a) The English language is better off than other languages. true ☐ false ☐

line(s) _____ : _____

_____

b) According to the author, one of today's most pressing challenges is the risk posed by the expanding digitalization of the world. true ☐ false ☐

line(s) _____ : _____

_____

c) The author promotes Globish as the language of the future. true ☐ false ☐

line(s) _____ : _____

_____

Total: ____/10 VP

Part B: Composition

ASSIGNMENT

The VDS (Verein Deutsche Sprache) wants the following article to be added to the German Constitution: "Die Sprache der Bundesrepublik Deutschland ist Deutsch"

(http://vds-ev.de/deutsch-in-der-politik/deutsche-sprache-ins-grundgesetz/deutsch-ins-grundgesetz/17.10.2017).

Discuss whether the German language needs to be protected by the German Constitution.

Part A: Comprehension – Solutions

ASSIGNMENTS

1. **Tick the correct answers (true/false).**

   a) The author cannot speak English. — false ☒
   line(s) 3 – 7: So it turns … the grey squirrel.

   b) American words and expressions have been integrated not only into the author's language, but into other people's languages as well. — true ☒
   line(s) 7 – 9: And I'm not … been similarly colonised.

   c) Americanisms can be more often found in the language of young people. — true ☒
   line(s) 11 – 13: In 2017, that … in a day".

2. **Tick the two correct statements.**

   According to the author, the reasons for the growing number of Americanisms in British English

   ☐ are America's increasing power.
   ☒ the simplicity of the American language.
   ☐ the indifference of the British people towards the changes their language is undergoing.
   ☒ the charm of American words and expressions.
   ☐ the flexibility of the English language.

   line(s) 20 – 22: … as America ascended … of quality control.
   line(s) 25: Sometimes, American words … seem more glamorous.

3. **Complete the following sentences using your own words or with words from the text.**

   a) According to the author, Esperanto **has failed to become a world language that all people share.**

   b) A country's words and expressions cannot be replaced by those of another country because **there will always be differences in the country's culture that must be expressed in their own language.**

4. **Tick the correct answers (true/false).**

   a) The English language is better off than other languages. — true ☒
   line(s) 42 – 43: It might seem … wiped out entirely.

   b) According to the author, one of today's most pressing challenges is the risk posed by the expanding digitalization of the world. — true ☒
   line(s) 43 – 45: But ultimately, the … global digital culture.

   c) The author promotes Globish as the language of the future. — false ☒
   line(s) 53 – 54: Personally, I … come to that.

Part B: Composition – Solutions

ASSIGNMENT

Students are expected
- to respect the rules of writing a comment, i. e. to introduce the topic under discussion, present arguments for and against, give examples, facts or figures and conclude by stating their own opinion on the topic, giving an outlook on future developments, presenting solutions.
- to explain the necessity of discussing whether the German language needs constitutional protection. They should point out that in the course of the ongoing process of globalization, English has in fact become a global language.
- As a consequence, English words and expressions can increasingly be found in the various languages of the world. With more and more English words and expressions being integrated into the original languages, some people consider English to be a threat to their native language.
- to state that this is the reason why they are calling for action to protect their language, e. g. by adding the article that German is the language of Germany to the Constitution.
- to present arguments for and against the protection of the German language, support their arguments with examples, facts and figures.

Arguments in favour might include:
- The language of a country is part of its cultural heritage. The loss of one's native language goes hand in hand with the loss of one's cultural identity.
- English words and expressions cannot substitute the original words and expressions of a language because each culture is unique and has aspects that cannot be properly described using foreign expressions.
- English as a global language generally endangers the diversity of the world's cultures, leading to the cultural homogenization of the world.

Arguments against may include:
- Languages have always undergone changes, e. g. have adopted words and expressions from other languages.
- English words and expressions are enriching/expanding, not replacing the German language.
- English is the language of communication in many fields, e. g. education, technology, science, international business, diplomacy.
- With nations, including Germany, increasingly developing into multicultural societies, English often serves as the only means of communication.

Appendix

Aufgabenarten und -formate

Listening Comprehension (Hörverstehen)

- Die Klausuren bestehen jeweils aus zwei verschiedenen Audiodokumenten.

Comprehension + Analysis/Mediation/Composition*

- Die Klausuren bestehen jeweils aus zwei Teilen, einem Leseverstehen *(Reading Comprehension)* und einer schriftlichen Textproduktion *(Analysis/Mediation/Composition)*.
- Das Leseverstehen geht mit 5 bzw. 10 Verrechnungspunkten in die Endbewertung ein.
- *Die schriftliche Textproduktion geht mit 25 Verrechnungspunkten in das Endergebnis ein, wobei 15 Verrechnungspunkte für die Sprache und 10 Verrechnungspunkte für den Inhalt gegeben werden.

Bewertungskriterien und Bewertungsraster

- Bewertungstabelle für Listening Comprehension (Hörverstehen)   88
- Kriterientabelle für die Vergabe von Verrechnungspunkten für die sprachliche Leistung   89
- Kriterientabelle für die Vergabe von Verrechnungspunkten für die inhaltliche Leistung   90
- Umrechnungstabelle von Verrechnungspunkten in Notenpunkte   91

---

* Die Bewertung sowohl des Leseverstehens und der schriftlichen Textproduktion als auch die Ermittlung der Endnote erfolgt auf der Grundlage der Beurteilungs- und Korrekturrichtlinien für moderne Fremdsprachen des Ministeriums für Kultus, Jugend und Sport Baden-Württemberg

Bewertungstabelle für Listening Comprehension (Hörverstehen)

Die Bewertung der Hörverstehensklausuren erfolgt nach folgender Tabelle*:

Verrechnungspunkte	Notenpunkte	Note
30 – 29	15	
28	14	sehr gut
27 – 26	13	
25	12	
24 – 23	11	gut
22	10	
21 – 20	9	
19	8	befriedigend
18 – 17	7	
16	6	
15 – 14	5	ausreichend
13	4	
12 – 11	3	
10	2	mangelhaft
9 – 8	1	
7 – 0	0	ungenügend

* Die Ermittlung der Endnote erfolgt auf der Grundlage der Notentabelle für Hörverstehensklausuren des Ministeriums für Kultus, Jugend und Sport Baden-Württemberg.

Kriterientabelle für die Vergabe von Verrechnungspunkten für die sprachliche Leistung

Verrechnungspunkte	Bewertungskriterien
sehr gute Leistung 15–13	• durchweg sehr gute Verständlichkeit, nahezu korrekter Sprachgebrauch; kaum Verstöße gegen die Sprachnorm • differenzierter Wortschatz, sichere Beherrschung von idiomatischen Wendungen • durchgehend differenzierter Gebrauch auch komplexer syntaktischer und grammatischer Strukturen • differenzierende funktionale Verwendung textstrukturierender Elemente
gute Leistung 12,5–10,5	• gute Verständlichkeit; weitgehend korrekter Sprachgebrauch; wenige Verstöße gegen die Sprachnorm • reichhaltiger und treffsicherer Wortschatz • weitgehend differenzierter Gebrauch auch komplexer syntaktischer und grammatischer Strukturen • funktionale Verwendung textstrukturierender Elemente
befriedigende Leistung 10–8,5	• die Verständlichkeit ist im Wesentlichen gegeben, angemessener Sprachgebrauch; mehrere Verstöße gegen die Sprachnorm • meist sichere Verwendung eines insgesamt einfacheren, dem Thema angemessenen Wortschatzes • durchgehend angemessener Gebrauch syntaktischer und grammatischer Strukturen • angemessene Verwendung textstrukturierender Elemente
ausreichende Leistung 8–5,5	• die Verständlichkeit ist stellenweise beeinträchtigt, noch angemessener Sprachgebrauch; viele Verstöße gegen die Sprachnorm • Verwendung eines einfachen, begrenzten Wortschatzes, der aber eine angemessene Darstellung des Sachverhaltes noch erlaubt • Gebrauch einfacher grammatischer Strukturen • textstrukturierende Elemente werden nur vereinzelt bzw. teilweise falsch verwendet
mangelhafte Leistung 5–2	• die Verständlichkeit ist deutlich beeinträchtigt, kaum noch angemessener Sprachgebrauch; sehr viele Verstöße gegen die Sprachnorm • Verwendung eines äußerst einfachen, sehr begrenzten Wortschatzes • Gebrauch äußerst einfacher, oft auch lückenhafter grammatischer Strukturen • fehlende bzw. häufig falsche Verwendung textstrukturierender Elemente
ungenügende Leistung 1,5–0	• eine Leistung, die der Aufgabenstellung nicht bzw. nur mit sehr großer Einschränkung gerecht wird

http://www.km-bw.de/site/pbs-bw-new/get/documents/KULTUS.Dachmandant/KULTUS/KM-Homepage/Artikelseiten%20KP-KM/Schularten/Gymnasium/Korrekturrichtlinien%202019.pdf (S. 46)

Kriterientabelle für die Vergabe von Verrechnungspunkten für die inhaltliche Leistung

Verrechnungspunkte	Bewertungskriterien
sehr gute Leistung 10 – 8,5	• erfüllt die gestellten Aufgaben umfassend • durchgehend sehr differenzierte, sachgerechte, logisch strukturierte und kohärente Darstellung • bei der Sprachmittlung werden gemäß der Aufgabenstellung alle relevanten Aspekte durchgängig klar und logisch strukturiert und gegebenenfalls umfassend adressatenbezogen wiedergegeben • die der Aufgabenstellung entsprechenden Textsortenmerkmale sind überzeugend angewandt
gute Leistung 8 – 7	• erfüllt die gestellten Aufgaben in allen wesentlichen Aspekten • differenzierte, sachgerechte, logisch strukturierte und kohärente Darstellung • bei der Sprachmittlung werden gemäß der Aufgabenstellung die relevanten Aspekte überwiegend klar und logisch strukturiert und gegebenenfalls mit dem erforderlichen Adressatenbezug wiedergegeben • die der Aufgabenstellung entsprechenden Textsortenmerkmale sind angemessen angewandt
befriedigende Leistung 6,5 – 5,5	• erfüllt die gestellten Aufgaben • weitgehend differenzierte, sachgerechte, logisch strukturierte und meist kohärente Darstellung • bei der Sprachmittlung werden gemäß der Aufgabenstellung die wichtigen Aspekte weitgehend strukturiert und entsprechend der Aufgabenstellung gegebenenfalls adressatenbezogen wiedergegeben • die der Aufgabenstellung entsprechenden Textsortenmerkmale sind meist angemessen angewandt
ausreichende Leistung 5 – 4	• erfüllt die gestellten Aufgaben in Grundzügen • insgesamt sachgerechte Darstellung, gewisse Mängel in der Strukturierung sowie in der Kohärenz • bei der Sprachmittlung werden die für die Aufgabenstellung notwendigen Aspekte wiedergegeben, teilweise Mängel in der Strukturierung, Kohärenz bzw. dem geforderten Adressatenbezug • die der Aufgabenstellung entsprechenden Textsortenmerkmale sind nicht durchgängig angemessen angewandt
mangelhafte Leistung 3,5 – 1,5	• erfüllt die gestellten Aufgaben nur eingeschränkt • nur wenig relevante Aspekte im Blick auf die Aufgabenstellung, Mängel in der sachgerechten Darstellung, Strukturierung und Kohärenz • bei der Sprachmittlung fehlen die für die Aufgabenstellung zentralen Aspekte; deutliche Mängel in der Strukturierung und im geforderten Adressatenbezug • die der Aufgabenstellung entsprechenden Textsortenmerkmale sind kaum erkennbar
ungenügende Leistung 1 – 0	• erfüllt die gestellten Aufgaben nicht bzw. nur mit sehr großer Einschränkung

http://www.km-bw.de/site/pbs-bw-new/get/documents/KULTUS.Dachmandant/KULTUS/KM-Homepage/Artikelseiten%20KP-KM/Schularten/Gymnasium/Korrekturrichtlinien%202019.pdf (S. 47)

Umrechnungstabelle von Verrechnungspunkten in Notenpunkte

Die Schülerinnen und Schüler können in den Klausuren insgesamt 30 oder 35 Verrechnungspunkte erlangen. Die Berechnung des Endergebnisses erfolgt auf der Grundlage folgender Tabelle:

Verrechnungspunkte 30	Verrechnungspunkte 35	Notenpunkte	Note
30 – 28,5	35 – 33,5	15	sehr gut
28 – 27	33 – 31,5	14	
26,5 – 25,5	31 – 29,5	13	
25 – 24	29 – 28	12	gut
23,5 – 22,5	27,5 – 26	11	
22 – 21	25,5 – 24,5	10	
20,5 – 19,5	24 – 22,5	9	befriedigend
19 – 18	22 – 21	8	
17,5 – 16,5	20,5 – 19	7	
16 – 15	18,5 – 17,5	6	ausreichend
14.5 – 13,5	17 – 15,5	5	
13 – 11	15 – 12,5	4	
10,5 – 8,5	12 – 10	3	mangelhaft
8 – 6	9 – 7	2	
5,5 – 3,5	6 – 4	1	
3 – 0	3 – 0	0	ungenügend

Acknowledgements

Images
|Cagle Cartoons, Santa Barbara, CA: Christo Komarnitski, Bulgaria 40. |Deutscher Caritasverband e. V., Berlin: 69. |iStockphoto.com, Calgary: baona 25.

Wir arbeiten sehr sorgfältig daran, für alle verwendeten Abbildungen die Rechteinhaberinnen und Rechteinhaber zu ermitteln. Sollte uns dies im Einzelfall nicht vollständig gelungen sein, werden berechtigte Ansprüche selbstverständlich im Rahmen der üblichen Vereinbarungen abgegolten.

Contents CD-ROM

 01_Audio

Track-Nr.	Klausur-Nr.	Dateiname (Material)	Laufzeit in min.
01	1	01_The Young Turks_Starbucks (The Young Turks: Starbucks End Controversial "Race Together" Campaign)	04:14
02	1	02_Obama_Selma Speech (Barack Obama: Selma Speech)	04:59
03	2	03_May_Lancaster House Speech_part 1 (Theresa May: Speech at Lancaster House)	04:32
04	2	04_May_Lancaster House Speech_part 2 (Theresa May: Speech at Lancaster House)	05:54

 02_Klausuren_pdf

Klausur-Nr.	Dateiname
1	01_Klausur.pdf
2	02_Klausur.pdf
3	03_Klausur.pdf
4	04_Klausur.pdf
5	05_Klausur.pdf
6	06_Klausur.pdf
7	07_Klausur.pdf
8	08_Klausur.pdf
9	09_Klausur.pdf
10	10_Klausur.pdf
11	11_Klausur.pdf
12	12_Klausur.pdf
13	13_Klausur.pdf
14	14_Klausur.pdf

 03_Klausuren_Word

Klausur-Nr.	Dateiname
1	01_Klausur.docx
2	02_Klausur.docx
3	03_Klausur.docx
4	04_Klausur.docx
5	05_Klausur.docx
6	06_Klausur.docx
7	07_Klausur.docx
8	08_Klausur.docx
9	09_Klausur.docx
10	10_Klausur.docx
11	11_Klausur.docx
12	12_Klausur.docx
13	13_Klausur.docx
14	14_Klausur.docx